T

PYJAMA

MYTH

THE
PYJAMA
MYTH

THE FREELANCE WRITER'S SURVIVAL GUIDE

SIAN MEADES-WILLIAMS

unbound

First published in 2022

Unbound
Level 1, Devonshire House, One Mayfair Place, London W1J 8AJ
www.unbound.com

Text design by PDQ Digital Media Solutions Ltd.

A CIP record for this book is available from the British Library

ISBN 978-1-80018-096-3 (paperback)
ISBN 978-1-80018-097-0 (ebook)

Printed in Great Britain by Clays Ltd, Elcograf S.p.A.

1 3 5 7 9 8 6 4 2

To all of the writers who haven't found the right words yet.

Contents

The First Word

This is a book about freelance writing.

It's a memoir, of sorts, but it's also a book about business. It's a practical guide. Break the spine, make notes, go at it with a highlighter, fold down pages. Make it yours.

It'll help you with pitching, guide you through the hard stuff – what to do about unpaid invoices, dealing with rejection and insecurity – and it will talk you through the nuts and bolts of making a business out of freelance writing. But our careers aren't just about the nuts and bolts. That's not the reason that we do what we do.

The Pyjama Myth will get to the heart of being a freelance writer. It's a book about success and how we define that. It will help you to explore what success really means to you, so you can navigate a freelance writing career that makes you truly happy. It'll help you carve a rewarding career that fuels every aspect of your life.

It took me years to realise that my success as a freelance writer wasn't just about article bylines or collecting commissions like Pokémon. If you follow the advice in this book – from me and from other hugely talented freelance writers and editors – you *will* get work with brilliant publications and clients that you love writing for, but I've learned that there's a lot more to building a lucrative and fulfilling freelance career. We need a stronger motivation to drive us.

Today, success is often defined by productivity. When someone asks how we are, we reply 'so busy!' without pause. We wear our tiredness like a badge of honour, dashing through our to-do lists. Busy means we're in demand. Busy *looks* like success, but if you measure success in these terms, it never comes – you're always reaching for something else. Something bigger, better, more, more, more. We are chasing an endless goal and we let our achievements fly right past us.

I used to measure my success by the number of clients I had, or by the flashy commissions that I could share on social media – I still get a kick from sharing work that I am proud of – but now I seek out clients that I gel with, companies that pay on time and editors I thoroughly enjoy working with.

My own definition of success is security – financial and emotional. It's in the freedom to take holidays and work when I like, and in no longer being in debt. It's feeling like I am in control of my own life. My life isn't grand or particularly lavish, but it's certainly not small.

My version of success will change throughout my life and my freelance writing career – and so will yours – but the feeling will stay the same. That even on the hardest days when everything is stacked against you, you still feel pretty damn lucky to get to write for a living. This book is about going after that feeling.

I asked some brilliant and talented freelance writers what their definition of success was, and their answers are peppered throughout the book. Every single writer gave a different answer. We're all motivated in different ways.

Success might look different to you, but I suspect you already know what it feels like. Do you enjoy writing for an hour on your lunch break while you carry on your full-time job? Maybe it allows you to move house to be closer to your family. Success can be about feeling brave (this book will help you to be brave). Your success could be setting aside time to write before the kids get home from school. Sometimes 400 words is all you need.

This is a book about freelance writing. It's a book about success.

It's a book about being happy.

Why 'The Pyjama Myth'?

When you go freelance, it will take approximately three seconds for someone to make a quip about you spending all day in your pyjamas. The thing is, sometimes it's true.

Huge chunks of this book were written in my pyjamas. Even if you are at your desk at nine every morning, your work outfit is going to be more relaxed than when you were in an office. You probably learned that during lockdown. There's a lot to be said for being comfortable with how we work.

Whether you go for striped flannel, silk piping, or a Hello Kitty T-shirt, the myth isn't that we sometimes wear pyjamas all day, it's that we can't be excellent, creative and talented writers while we're wearing them.

'That's not how I do it...'

Despite my writing 60,000 words on the topic, freelancing doesn't come with hard and fast rules. The fact that there's no one-size-fits-all approach is part of the appeal – but there can be a wrong way to go about things. Like that time that I panic-pitched seven ideas to the same editor after I lost a huge client. Or when I was so worried about paying my rent that I pitched a piece when I was getting sick and then I wasn't well enough to file on time. These are fine examples of doing the wrong thing.

All freelance writers work differently, and that doesn't necessarily mean that you're doing it wrong. I'm not here to tell you that the way you work is crap. Every freelance writer has their own way, and every editor has their own preferences. What worked for you a year ago may not be right for you now. What works for one client could jar with another. I want to help you improve what *isn't* working for you, so that you don't get in your own way. You might have incredible results when you're going against the grain or ignoring all the advice that you're offered and often *that's* the right way to do things. Pick and choose what works for you, mix it up with what you already know. Create your own special brand of freelance success.

From pitching and invoicing to juggling deadlines and feedback, every freelancer and editor I spoke to while I was writing this book had their own way of working. They all agreed on certain points, though – sticking to deadlines, working to the brief, being consistent; those points came up time and time again. If you do things differently to the advice in this book and it works for you, I am thrilled for you. I'm not about to suggest that you change that. But if writing starts to feel like more of a struggle than it used to, or your pitches aren't turning into commissions, then it's time to switch things up.

There is an abundance of information in this book, as well as practical exercises to get you working with pen and paper. Please don't let yourself be overwhelmed. Making a success of freelance writing doesn't happen overnight. You can't 'complete' this book.

Don't worry if you flip ahead and feel out of your depth. You'll get there in your own time. Giant leaps feel great, but there's a reason I write so much about good habits and solid foundations. They may not sound very exciting but they're vital. Hopefully they'll stop you falling flat on your arse like I did in my early years.

The path your freelance writing career takes won't be anything like you imagined. Freelancing is most exciting when you say yes to new ideas and unexpected projects. This is how I launched *Domestic Sluttery* – the lifestyle website that cemented my career. It's why I started the media industry newsletter *Freelance Writing Jobs*. It's the reason you're holding this crowdfunded book in your hands (thank you, Unbound supporters!) and it's why the Freelance Writing Awards were created in 2021. I hope you'll open yourself up to new ways of working, so when an unexpected opportunity comes – be it travel, interviews, a feature commission you had never dreamed of – you're ready for it.

The Pyjama Myth isn't a do-or-die list of rules (how boring that would be) and it's not a cheat's guide – there's no life hack with this job. You'll craft the ideas, write the pitches, chase the invoices (and then chase them again), and take the steps towards something great. The hard work will be all yours. So will the successes.

Getting Started

I'm not going to tell you to quit your day job.

Making the jump into full-time freelance life might work for you, or it might not. This book isn't about to tell you to pack up your current life and become a full-time freelance writer if that's not the right choice for you. Many writers freelance on the side of their day jobs, and they do it brilliantly. Being a successful freelance writer is about finding a way of freelancing that works for you, and if that's writing on Fridays or pitching an article every so often around childcare, this way of freelancing is just as valid as someone who earns their income from writing every day.

The idea that there's one way to become a freelance writer is a myth. Even if you do opt to make it your full-time career, there's no single way in through a big gate. Some of you will make the jump from a staff writer position after you've spent a few months building up some savings. Or you might have gathered so much freelance work alongside your full-time job that you need to make the leap before you run yourself ragged. You could be finishing up your degree and wondering what to do next. And you may not have a choice in the matter: redundancy from traditional media staff jobs is a huge reason many writers go down the freelance route – in a report by the Association of

Independent Professionals and the Self-Employed (IPSE) in 2020, 19% of freelancers across all industries say that job losses were a factor in their decision to become self-employed.[1] Parenthood is certainly another reason – IPSE's research has shown that in the UK there were over 300,000 freelance mums in 2020. That means 14% of the total freelance population – one in seven – are working mothers.[2]

Traditional employment doesn't always welcome returning parents – specifically mothers – with open arms, so freelancing can be an appealing solution for working around children. One of the biggest reasons for the growth in self-employment figures since 2008 is women choosing to follow the self-employed career path – 63% of women said that the decision to go freelance was to give them greater control of their hours, and 55% of women in the report were looking for a better work-life balance.[3] Being able to work around family and childcare plays a big part in the decision to freelance.

It's clear that money isn't necessarily the driving force in the reason for the cultural shift, but while every writer's reason for choosing to freelance is different, there is still one common factor: **we want to take control of our careers.**

We want our careers to fit around the rest of our lives, to suit our needs personally as well as professionally. Freelancing allows that *and* we don't waste our entire lunch breaks standing in the queue at the post office.

The first section of this book is about setting yourself up so you're ready for the challenges that freelance life will throw at you. Even if you're a seasoned freelancer, those challenges can surprise you. Being prepared won't stop a curveball from being lobbed in your direction, but it could stop you getting hit square in the face. We'll cover the basics – like taking care of your brain and body, and setting up some systems and structure to your workday so you feel on top of everything. We'll also try to answer broader questions to establish what's driving you to be a freelance writer. These things are your safety net – whenever freelancing gets tough, I always go back to the basics.

So, let's start right at the beginning. My own journey into freelance writing was, frankly, an arse-backwards way to go about things.

I began freelancing accidentally. I was about to turn twenty-five and in my second job out of university – selling advertising for an in-flight magazine. I was trying to sneak into the magazine industry through the back door and I'd actually promised in my interview that although I had been dabbling with writing in my spare time, I had no intention of writing becoming a full-time career. It wasn't a total lie: until that interview it hadn't even occurred to me that my hobby could lead to something more than writing on weekends.

I had graduated just before the world went truly digital – research for my English literature degree was done in an internet café down the road from the dodgy estate I lived on. We stood in line to submit our essays on *paper*. Everything was online within a year of me graduating. The internet wasn't new, but that cusp of digital becoming mainstream culture was something special and I feel incredibly lucky that my writing career was at the start of it. People were trying new things, fooling around on the internet, starting something. It was a great thing to be a part of. An unusual chain of events led to me getting offered a freelance gig; I needed to take a chunk of time off work after coming down with a horrible virus. The recovery was much slower than I'd expected, and while I wasn't well enough to walk for longer than five minutes, I could sit in bed and I could write. So I did. Every day for a month.

It felt dishonest to be writing when I couldn't work full-time, but I'd watched every DVD and I'd read every book I owned. There was little else to do while I recovered. When an editor got in touch about some paying work for Yahoo, I got the gig and juggled both the project and my full-time job. I had started freelance writing without realising.

Soon after, another job followed: this time as an editor of a new website about London. I needed to leave my full-time job. I probably should have thought twice about it, but of course I didn't. I was being offered a chance at something, and I was young enough to say yes without stopping to be scared by the prospect. When you're twenty-four, you say yes to things and figure them out later.

Suddenly I was freelance and editing a lifestyle website with very little experience for very little money. I wasn't ready for such an undertaking; I had no experience interviewing people, and I didn't even know how to make a content plan. As you can probably imagine, my shiny new job lasted all of three months. I realise now that I wasn't given the support for things to have panned out any other way.

Blind optimism and arrogance carried me through my first few years of freelancing (and if I'm honest, they still do sometimes), but there was something else at work, too: despite the fact I had built up a good number of writing samples and had some pretty solid writing experience, for some reason I was still convinced that I wouldn't be able to get a staff writing job. (I believe the reason we're looking for here is low self-esteem.) I didn't even throw my hat in the ring. I was incredibly lucky that my South-East London rent was peanuts (although less lucky about the mouse infestation). Without that cushion, I suspect I would have returned home to Shropshire.

Instead, I begged and badgered everyone I knew for contacts and work. A friend suggested I speak to one of his editors and, amazingly, I cobbled together a pretty good semblance of a pitch despite having no idea if I was doing it right. That piece didn't get picked up, but the editor commissioned me to write a different piece later that week, about the rise of burlesque clubs in London (look, it was 2007, OK?). That commission changed my life. Thank you, Stewart Who?.

Suddenly I was sitting in my dirt-cheap mouse-riddled house in South London and £400 richer for writing something that I was proud of.

I knew it right then. This was what I wanted to do.

When your first-ever pitch leads to a commission, there's only one thing you can hear inside your head: this is going to be so easy!

Reader, it was not easy.

'But I'm not a real freelance writer!'

Not everyone feels like a 'real' freelance writer when they start out. Maybe you've got 'aspiring' in your Twitter bio, or you only talk about your writing with your close friends. This is my third book and I still pause before calling myself an author. Whether you split your time between writing features and doing social media for a sock brand, or write beauty articles from 8 a.m. to 2 p.m. before picking your kids up from school, it's easy for people to tell you that you're 'not a real freelance writer'. I'm here to tell you that it's all rubbish.

Your freelance writing will be different to everyone else's. You might focus on business writing and trade publications or love your part-time copywriting job that pays for you to go on holiday each year. Your freelance writing work, in whatever form it takes, is valid. You do not have to be writing long reads or opinion pieces in national newspapers to call yourself a freelance writer.

On Valentine's Day in 2018, I launched a weekly newsletter called *Freelance Writing Jobs*, which does exactly what it says on the tin. I share a curated collection of brilliant freelance writing jobs and calls for pitches. All paying, all in the UK. Over 27,000 writers subscribe and every year it makes them hundreds of thousands of pounds in commissions and paying work. The email features every kind of writing imaginable – copywriting, magazine commissions, social media, editorial content for brands, writing website copy. You might find yourself doing a mix of all of these things in your writing career. It's *all* freelance writing.

My work is connected in so many unexpected ways. My product copywriting for furniture and fashion companies helped me hone my newsletter-writing skills. My lifestyle newsletter *Tigers Are Better Looking* is the reason I've landed feature commissions, books and copywriting gigs. If you think there's only one way to make a living as a freelance writer, then let me tell you now: you are missing out and someone else will gladly eat that slice of pie for you.

'Not a real freelance writer' is a statement that is aimed to diminish someone's work and I have no time for it. Freelancing is not a secret club and nothing is gained if we treat it like one. There's no special handshake. If you are hired to write words for a particular project, and you get paid for them, you're a freelance writer.

There was a time when the most typical way of freelancing was writing articles and getting paid for them, but things look different these days. This is in part because of dwindling freelance journalism rates, but the potential and variety in writing careers today is one of the joys of freelancing. You might find that you love writing social media copy for travel companies. Perhaps your talent for short-form editorial extends into copywriting for your favourite shoe brand. I've dabbled in video script writing, and I know several writers who work in TV and podcast writing alongside their articles. There's no one way to be a freelance writer.

You are a freelance writer if:

- You make your entire living pitching and writing articles.
- Yesterday you decided to go freelance full-time.
- You sent your first pitch to a magazine editor ten minutes ago.
- You decide to try freelancing when you've finished reading this book.
- You got paid to do the copy for your brother's plumbing business. Or your best mate's jewellery business.
- You're writing copy for drinks companies through a creative agency.
- You're working a full-time job and falling asleep at your desk because you stayed up until 1 a.m. writing an article you pitched that you were convinced you'd finish before the end of *Project Runway*.
- You did article edits on your lunch break while getting soup down your shirt.

- You spend your weekends writing for different outlets, but you aren't ready to leave your job just yet.
- You write a newsletter that makes money through subscriptions, reader donations or advertising.
- You had one commission from an editor, and you write article ideas on your phone but haven't pitched them yet because it scares you.

This is the bottom line: you are a freelance writer when you decide to be one.

We need to talk about the pandemic

As I began writing this book in March 2020, Coronavirus was just starting to make headlines in the UK. The world was going into lockdown and very quickly the media industry changed irreversibly. Freelance writers saw their regular jobs slashed, commissioning budgets vanished overnight and millions of self-employed people found themselves left without any government assistance. The rug was pulled out from under us all.

There's a large gap of time between writing the first draft of a book and its actual publication date – the situation I'm writing about now will be completely different by the time this book is in your hands. It's incredibly hard to predict what will happen next when you're still in the middle of something. I submitted the first draft of this book in January 2021. We were still in lockdown. News had just broken that over 100,000 people in the UK had died from the virus. It's incredibly hard to extrapolate this tragedy and think about the future, or something as comparatively everyday as work. And yet we must, because we keep going. What is true, and will be true even after it's over, is that we have never faced anything like this before. Coronavirus will define our lives in ways we cannot yet comprehend and it's impossible to say what impact this will have on us. A huge part of that impact centres around our work lives and our financial futures. The devastation and collective grief are insurmountable.

So I look for things that fill me with hope. I have to seek them out and pull them into focus, otherwise it's too easy to feel helpless and entirely overwhelmed. Despite the huge, immediate challenges for the media industry, new publications began in the middle of everything. Writers started their own newsletters. Projects that had been lingering in the background made their way to the fore because writers had more time to focus on their own creativity. Sometimes this was through lack of work, sometimes it was just to kill the endless days that blurred into each other. None of this can reassure the writers who lost their jobs, or the self-employed who found themselves excluded from the government's grants. The new publications bring with them something wonderful, but they don't replace what was so brilliant about the ones that the industry lost. Nevertheless, we persisted.

The pandemic stretched publications in ways they couldn't have prepared for. Media companies also realised just how crucial freelancers can be to a business. Writing isn't a skill that can be replicated easily; it's a craft that takes time and it's one that is always worth paying for. Freelance writers offer something unique.

What the pandemic did was add incredible levels of pressure. Even simple tasks that we usually enjoyed suddenly became a challenge. Making dinner was as hard as pitching a story, gathering up the energy to write 800 words felt like climbing a mountain. There was no rhyme or reason to how lockdown felt – as soon as I thought I'd got the measure of things, I found myself sobbing into my tea later the same day. Freelancers are used to working from home, but it certainly wasn't 'business as usual'. Everyone struggled in their own way. I needed therapy.

Change is something that the media industry is used to, although we don't usually notice it so starkly. Two world wars, the arrival of the internet, the financial crisis, the boom of social media. All of these events have changed our media landscape. What's next? An opportunity for reform, I hope. And repair.

What I have been certain of through all of this is that freelancers have a huge capacity for resilience. It can get battered and bruised, it can get trampled on, but I don't know a group of people who fight back like freelancers do. Even on our worst days, we go out on our own and negotiate contracts, deal with rejection, chase unpaid invoices, and still find time to write brilliant articles. Then, after a cup of tea (and perhaps a bit of a cry), some of you will schedule an interview, create award-winning copy and manage a fridge forage all before 4 p.m. Freelancers are used to dealing with dozens of things at once, but what's most impressive is the huge array of simultaneous emotions that a freelancer can juggle. We talk about highs and lows in business; there are times we're dealing with commissions and rejections in the same breath.

We wear our resilience like a medal, but we shouldn't have to. It's not a badge to be earned. It doesn't make us better than anyone else, or more talented. It makes us more susceptible to anxiety and burnout. The simple truth is that during lockdown, freelancers weren't supported enough by the government. Millions weren't supported at all. Being resilient might be something to be proud of, but it shouldn't be what we're aiming for. We deserve better.

None of us know what will happen next week, next month, next year. Our world and our life alter in ways that we cannot fathom. We will always need people to help us make sense of it all, and to help others find strength and comfort in words. Whatever challenges the media industry faces, writers do that. You do that.

What's your 'why'?

There's something unique that drives every freelance writer. Something outside of the actual words. Is it freedom to choose your own projects? Is it using your voice to highlight a particular issue? The ability to make your own money with no ceiling on your earnings? Is it a job that you can do at 3 a.m. between feeds?

All freelance writers have their 'why'.

Your 'why' isn't always easy to define, but it should become the thing that drives what you do, because when you're focused on the reason behind it, the small choices you make are for a bigger reason.

If you haven't figured out your 'why', you'll feel like you're that hamster on the wheel, just writing and writing but feeling like you've achieved very little. When you're having a crappy day where nothing is coming together and everything you write is clunky, knowing your 'why' helps you feel more settled. It keeps you going.

Every goal I set, everything I follow through on, needs a 'why' driving it. If I don't have one, I often discover that I'm chasing something pretty flimsy, or pitching for something that doesn't serve me anymore. I wish I'd figured out sooner that I didn't actually *want* to learn to play the guitar in my twenties, I just wanted to kiss boys who did. I spent a decade feeling guilty about the guitar that came with me to every flat I rented, gathering dust in the corner.

Whenever I've forgotten my 'why', my goals gather dust, too. I'll stop writing for myself. I'll take jobs that don't get me excited. My motivations feel off, I choose to work with clients that I know are going to be difficult. I forget myself. Occasionally when I see my peers being so brilliant at something, I start pushing myself towards what I think I 'should' be going for. It's hard not to follow someone else's path to success when you see it going so well for them. Those writers are knocking it out of the park because they know what their 'why' is, and it's probably different to yours.

When you figure out what your 'why' is, keep focused on it. Hold it as close as you can and always have it in your mind. It's what will drive you to make the decisions that are right for you.

Making the jump

I promised that I wasn't going to tell you to quit your job and I'm still not going to. However, for those of you who are on the cusp of making the jump to freelancing full-time, and who have considered it more than once in the last ten minutes, month or even the last year, there are some things to think about before you make the leap. Before you rush to hand in your notice, ask yourself the following questions:

Are you freelancing more than twenty hours a week and still working full-time?
Most of us can do a little bit of something on the side of a full-time job. Whether it's writing a novel, starting a newsletter (for

more on side projects, turn to page 158) or finally finishing your Zelda game, there's usually a little bit of time to play with. When you start freelance writing there can be an overlap because you're essentially doing two jobs at once. There is only so long you can do this before your work starts to suffer – either your full-time job or your freelance projects.

Are you spending your lunch breaks doing freelance admin?

Invoicing, sharing articles on Twitter, working on edits for someone else. You're not strictly writing on another company's time, but managers dislike it when work outside of the office gets brought to your desk. You're probably not being as subtle as you think so it pays to consider the message you're sending to your boss and your colleagues. Grab your laptop and take yourself to a nice café for a solo working lunch.

Are you sacrificing your weekends *and* evenings?

It is entirely your call when you work, and there will always be times you need to put the hours into a project, but we all need some downtime. If you're working more than you're relaxing, you're going to burn out. And you're not giving yourself the chance to do your best work.

Have you achieved everything you want to in your current job?

It's OK to wait for the right time. If you've got a big event that you'd like to see through to the end, or you want to build up experience in a particular area before you feel you're ready to go it alone, do these things! You don't have to 'launch' your freelance career. There's no date that you have to go freelance by, and goodness me it is not and never has to be before you're thirty.

19

Are you planning on buying a house in the near future?

While it's untrue that freelancers can't get a mortgage, you do have more hoops to jump through and you will find it very difficult to get a mortgage without two years of filed tax returns (some mortgage providers ask for three). If you were planning on putting a deposit down in the next year, it might be worth sticking at your full-time job until you've got the keys to your new home.

Are you ready?

This is the big one. It might well be why you bought this book. You know when you're ready even though it feels scary. You just need a plan for the next steps.

Still not sure if freelance writing is for you? Here's the big freelance secret: you don't have to be a freelance writer for the rest of your life. It is not an irreversible decision. I love being a freelance writer enough to write a whole book about it but I've still had a couple of full-time stints in my career.

If you find that you hate freelancing, or you get a full-time offer that you just can't pass up, know this: you can always change your mind. You can always change it back again, too. You haven't failed in any way. Being freelance is always about having a choice, and making the decision to *not* do something is incredibly brave.

> ### Freelance success story
> *'I feel successful as a freelance writer when it's three o'clock on a Tuesday afternoon and I'm in my kitchen making a cake, or walking on the beach, or sitting in an empty cinema. Life is short, and I chose this job so that I can enjoy it on my terms, by being a weekday gallivanter whenever I want.*

When I worked in an office, I wondered if I would have the discipline to be a freelancer: to get up early, type my heart out, eat a hearty lunch and knock off every weekend. But then I realised that isn't the point of freelancing for me. It's about carving out time for life's pleasures by working around them. I'll write on a Saturday in exchange for a Monday spent with my best friend, or stay up late to finish a feature if it means pottering in the garden the next morning. When I can say yes to fun and no to drudgery, that's success.' **Laura Brown, freelance writer and my co-editor of lifestyle newsletter** Tigers Are Better Looking

Do you need money in the bank?

There's a pearl of wisdom about freelancing that says you shouldn't make the jump until you've got enough money in savings to cover you for six months. That's your safety net. It's your security.

On the face of it, this sounds like good advice. Savings make life much easier, and a safety net can take the pressure off significantly. However, that suggested figure is a huge amount of money. Conservatively, it's five grand. If I'd tried to save that when I was twenty-four, it just wouldn't have happened. In the early years I lived month to month, figuring it out as I went along. It took me years to get a handle on my savings.

Suggesting that you need a six-month pot before you make the change keeps freelance writing accessible only to a certain group of writers. A certain class of writers. Talented writers who are working on minimum wage, living on the breadline, or getting paid weekly, just don't get a look-in. It makes a freelance career feel unattainable. It keeps the door shut.

Rather than a nice big cash pot that will cover you for six months, it's better to start paying into an emergency fund as a matter of priority when you begin freelancing. This pot is there if you get sick, or you just need to take a few weeks off unexpectedly – caring for a relative, needing to move at short notice. An emergency fund stops you getting so stressed out about money that you can't do your job. You know your life, so you get to decide how much this fund needs to be. It might start at £100 or an even grand. It could be the amount your mortgage and bills cost each month. Whatever your figure, it's there to help you, not to stress you out because you're saving so much that you can't live your life.

What would you lose if your best-paying client didn't pay you on time? What's in jeopardy if that happens? Your emergency fund should cover the things that you can't afford to lose. When you've got a figure in mind, you can start saving towards that. This option is so much better than an arbitrary figure plucked out of the air.

We are bad at talking about money, and we frequently talk about savings negatively – we're told we should be saving for a rainy day, but that we shouldn't dip into them. I've been warned against using my savings my whole life, but they are there when we need them, otherwise what's the point? It's not a contest to see how much you can squirrel away. Having an emergency fund gives you freedom. You don't need one before you make the jump, but you'll be incredibly thankful that you worked towards one. Just like you probably won't win a Pulitzer in your first week as a freelancer, your savings pot won't fill up overnight, but every choice – however small – that you make to improve your freelance future is a good one.

Know where you're starting from

What does your first day as a freelance writer look like? Unlike starting a new full-time job, there's no set agenda. You might already have a client or two lined up, or half a dozen commissions on the go. Maybe you've taken the leap without having any of that in your back pocket and you're staring at a blank page. It will probably include a Twitter announcement (excellent GIF choice, by the way). You'll definitely have bought a new notebook and may have even created a lovely email signature. You've had a healthy breakfast and you've got your cuppa in your favourite mug.

No matter how prepared you've been for this day, you will not feel ready. The night before my first proper freelance day I had slept in a supposedly haunted plague pit under London Bridge, so while there's no way of feeling totally prepared, do learn from my mistakes and avoid all plague-pit-and-red-wine sleepovers. I did not see any ghosts.

The only other thing you can do is embrace the lack of structure, go at your own pace and try and determine where you're starting from.

If you've got one copywriting client when you start your first morning, adding 'TEN NEW CLIENTS!!!' to your daily to-do list is going to be a bit of a stretch. That's not to say that these things can't happen – please, please shoot for the stars – but managing your own expectations can help you feel in control. You don't have to complete every single career goal by 3 p.m. Especially not in your first couple of weeks, when you're getting used to everything and trying to figure out your new schedule and work rhythms (the novelty of the mid-morning wank does wear off after a while). Be realistic about where you're starting from and what you need to do next. Do you want to send more feature pitches or perhaps work on a book? Is your aim to bag more copywriting work? Did you finish that article that's already on your to-do list?

You get to plan your first day as a freelancer. And the next one. And the one after that. The only way that you can do that and enjoy it is to go at your own pace. Again, we come back to the cult of busy. Just because you can do 101 tasks before midday doesn't mean that you need to. Start with the most important and time-sensitive tasks on your list. And then stop for lunch.

The freelance diet

I think about food a lot.

I love to cook, I regularly write about food, and reading restaurant menus even if I don't have a reservation is a legitimate hobby that my husband Tom calls 'peruse bouching'. Yet I often eat lunch at 4 p.m. and that 'lunch' is often cereal.

I see food as the ultimate joy, which can be a dangerous reward system when you work for yourself. 'I'll just finish this article and then I'll make lunch!' sounds great in theory but then it's 3 p.m. and you're furiously bashing at your keyboard and writing words that you will only delete later.

It's easy for your diet to be all over the place when you work from home. 'I don't have time to make anything!' you wail, staring forlornly at the smidgen of peanut butter that you just ate from your finger.

Even if you enjoy pottering about in the kitchen and embracing an elaborate lunch as a glorious form of procrastination, on a day-to-day basis your desk lunches are likely to be pretty basic. Sometimes it's too hard to think about another meal in the middle of the workday. You may even find yourself missing the convenience of a certain sandwich chain. So here's a short list of basic freelance lunches. None of this is rocket science – you don't need me to tell you how to boil an egg – and it's definitely not fine dining. It's just about making sure you remember to eat when work takes over and you need to fuel your body and brain to keep going.

Instant noodles

You can pimp instant noodles with so much good stuff – leftover roast chicken, a soft-boiled egg, chilli flakes, that spice mix you bought on a whim.

Supermarket soups

When you have a lavish enough lunch window that you can actually eat a metre away from your laptop, supermarket soups are surprisingly good. Go for Heinz when you need a cosy treat.

Freezer roulette

Every time you cook dinner, pop a single portion in the freezer. You'll be thankful for it when you're sick of eating toast. Make sure you label each portion, otherwise you'll serve yourself a bowl of onion gravy.

Baking potatoes

Whack one in the oven at eleven and you'll be so pleased with yourself at lunchtime. I remember to do this only once a month.

Eggs eight billion ways

You *do* have time to fry an egg. You have time to scramble an egg. You even have time to make an omelette. You probably don't have time to learn how to poach an egg. Eggs save many a freelance afternoon, and in the case of dippy eggs and soldiers will be just what you wanted.

Things on bread

Toast is the freelance diet staple. Flatbreads, bagels, sliced white with whatever happens to be in your fridge slathered on top. Cream cheese, marmalade, hot sauce. And, a full week after you've bought it, that ripe 'n' ready avocado.

Cheese

Burrata on fancy sourdough, cheese on crackers (very Christmassy), cheese on toast, a hunk of posh cheddar while you're standing by the fridge. Dairylea triangles. All acceptable freelance lunches.

Cereal

There will be some days when you actually *are* too busy to consider making a piece of toast. The answer here is a bowl of Crunchy Nut Cornflakes. You always have time for a bowl of cereal. On these days I also avoid endless mugs of cold tea by making up a desk Thermos. If you only take one tip from this book, I hope it's this one.

Crisps

Don't you judge me.

When I need something a little more substantial but easy, I turn to *SIMPLE* by Diana Henry, or Ed Smith's *On the Side*, which as the name suggests is about side dishes, but whack them next to some bread and you've got a brilliant lunch. These cookbooks are so good at making the contents of your fridge look exciting very quickly.

There will be times when your lunches are in cute cafés, or from the nice little place on the corner. Occasionally other people will pay for lunch, and you'll dip nice bread in olive oil that costs more than your train ticket and feel very Professional Freelance Writer all the way home. When I've got a big deadline looming, I stock up on noodles and make sure I've got potato waffles in the freezer. Anything to stop lunch turning into a big drama which means I cry about my deadline and have to settle for an average takeaway at 10 p.m. No matter how much work you have on your plate, your brain and body deserve better than that sad little scenario.

Taking care of your body

I'm writing this sitting in bed.

Rain is driving against the window, and I can't quash my hankering for cosiness. And, let's be honest, laziness. That I've stumbled upon a career I can do dressed any way I like, anywhere I like, feels like I've pulled off an amazing trick.

I also know that writing in bed is one of the worst things I do for myself in my day-to-day freelance life.

It's so easy to forget about taking care of your body when you're freelance. It's especially easy in your twenties. Writing in bed is a habit I've taken with me from poky bedrooms in shared flats, avoiding awful housemates. We hunch over our words on benches, trains, beaches, plane seats on long-haul flights. It's hardly surprising that writing brings with it terrible posture and,

27

if we're not careful, endless back problems. When I was twenty-five, I could get away with it without so much as a twinge. Now? Not so much.

When you work in an office, this is figured out for you – your desk setup needs to be suitable to sit at for eight hours. Your office chair was springy, you probably had a nice wrist support. Unless you've invested in a proper workspace, your options are the nearest table – yours or a local café's – the sofa or cosying up in bed. Or the 'soft office' as my Freelance Writing Awards partner Anna Codrea-Rado likes to call it. In winter, working under a duvet is practical – I can't write if I can't feel my fingers.

Our daily habits have a long-term impact on our bodies. I suffer from RSI in my wrist due to using the trackpad on my laptop so frequently. All that cutting and pasting and whizzing around the internet has come back to bite me.

We don't notice it when we're working from home, but we stop moving. Those five minutes that we'd take to go and see Hannah three desks down is replaced with a tweet. We don't need to go out and get lunch, we've got our leftovers from yesterday. We could have a well-deserved break with a walk around the block or we could watch an episode of *Murder, She Wrote* and eat a Twix. We don't stretch our bodies and our dining chair isn't the best option for eight hours of editing, even with the fancy cushion.

Our sleeping patterns will be off – it's easy to get in the habit of staying up super late, safe in the knowledge that no one is going to tell you off if you're not at your desk by 9.30 a.m. I'm a night owl, so I don't often start work before 9 a.m. I'm OK with that most of the time but not when I can't get going because I keep working past midnight. I stop enjoying work and my editors aren't getting the best out of me.

None of this just happens one day. That old adage about habits being daily choices that we make is absolutely true in this case. It could take years for you to notice the impact that working from home can have on your body. It's incredibly hard to consciously keep track of everything – this is why some companies have entire departments to take care of employee well-being and safety.

I'm not suggesting that you need to schedule a workout every morning or your freelance life will forever be a mess and your body will go to shit. I'm suggesting that you take care of yourself even when no one is around to make sure you do it. There's something wonderfully regressive about working from home – that behaviour that you get into when you've got the house to yourself for the night? Working from home can feel similar. You revert to what feels good and that doesn't necessarily mean what's good for you.

I know that I'll never stop working from under my duvet. I've got a perfectly good office chair, but I like being super comfy when I'm doing my research. There's absolutely nothing sexy about my orthopaedic cushions, but they give better lower back support and it feels like a halfway solution. It's not perfect, but it is better. And I'll take that.

Not everything we enjoy is good for us. I'm never going to stop eating fried chicken and I still smoke the odd cigarette after three pints. Taking care of your body may come naturally to you, but for some it will be harder and that's alright. Doing what you can is always better than doing nothing at all. The fact remains that you *do* need to take care of your body however you can. You are responsible for it. This is true for all of us, at all ages, but especially when you work for yourself. Because you don't get sick pay.

When you're not getting sick pay, the stakes are higher. I don't say this to admonish anyone, but I kick myself for not always taking the proper precautions to protect my wrist. The time off has cost me thousands of pounds in lost freelance work. There's no one to take over writing that feature when you're high as a kite on painkillers. So you need to do what you can. Or at least try and meet your body halfway. Ignoring that twinge is ignoring the warning that your body is giving you. Do what you can when you can and try to be conscious of the point when you stop being conscious of it. Now I run when I've met a deadline and do my best to end the day with yoga, which is nothing short of witchcraft for back pain. I try and remember to drink water, but it never feels like enough. You can't aim for perfection; you don't deserve the guilt of that when you fall short.

When you take small steps to make your body feel better, work feels much easier. You can pull an all-nighter when you need to, you can take on projects that are more demanding. It can feel glib to say that small things help. If you have a disability or a chronic health condition, sometimes it's not that simple. Sometimes your body fights against you. So we find things that work for us, and make our work life as comfortable and manageable as possible. We do what we can.

I play video games far less these days, and very rarely when I'm working to a deadline – I need to take care of my wrist. I've also made my peace with occasional cosy mornings in bed if I run regularly (and slowly). The compromises you make will vary – what you're able to do with your body might be very different to other freelance writers. If you're hiding in your bedroom to avoid housemates, remembering to go out for a walk or stretching at your desk every hour can help beyond measure. I'm realistic about my lack of inclination around my physical health, but I wish it was at the forefront of my mind more often. There are some things in freelancing that are out of our control, but taking care of our body is something we can choose to improve, even in the smallest of ways.

Take care of your mental health

This isn't a self-help book. I'm not a qualified coach, I'm not a therapist. However, when we spend roughly eight hours a day working, it's impossible for our mental health and professional life to be separate. Our self-care is being squished into weekends and days off. When you are literally your own business, your work and mental well-being are even more tangled together.

Everything I do in my freelance day, every decision I make, every commission I accept or reject, boils down to asking myself one question: will this be good for my mental health? This isn't a lovely Instagram-modified version of self-care, it's literally how I ensure I take care of my brain.

If my brain is having a tough time, *I can't work.* I don't always make the right choices. I don't eat enough greens, and I take on too much and I stop running because I'm too busy to pull my trainers on. The first thing to suffer when I'm not taking care of myself isn't my body, it's my mind. I feel flat, I have no energy, I don't get excited about my work, I sleep for hours but I still feel groggy. Even if I can do the work, I can't engage with it. I hate working like this.

It's hard to talk about mental health in general terms – there isn't one approach that works for everyone, and I can't tell you the steps you need to put in place to keep your own mental health on track. Working from home and working

31

for yourself are often sold as a silver bullet, the thing that is here to save us from the trials and tribulations of modern life. 'Go freelance! It's great for mental health!' is the message that people so frequently peddle. And it's a big misconception. Being freelance doesn't make your mental health issues vanish. It can even swing the other way – when you don't have the routine of a full-time job to stick to, mental health problems can come into the light.

Of course, there are some elements of working for yourself that can improve your mental health – being able to drop work in the middle of the afternoon and get some fresh air is certainly one of them (so is sneaking off to the cinema on your own, FYI) – but there are also downsides that aren't often addressed. You exercise less – don't underestimate how many daily steps you'd rack up running around an office or commuting to work. As we've already discussed, you eat weirdly. You work odd hours and will sometimes feel like you always have to be 'on', which means you're replying to emails while you're watching Netflix. You get lazy about your appearance and skip morning showers when you have no meetings. The line between your home and work life gets fuzzy, and that can be mentally exhausting for a lot of people.

On a professional level, you also lose your immediate community, and with it the reassurance that you're doing a good job. That validation doesn't always arrive nicely packaged when you're freelance. You might just get a 'thank you!' or 'love it!' from an editor, but often you don't hear back about your work unless there's a problem or something needs editing. In a typical work environment, we're used to being told when we've done a good job, or there's a celebration cake on a Friday. It can be a big change to juggle half a dozen projects and have no one tell you that you're doing OK. You're the one that has to tell yourself that you're doing well. You're the one who has to celebrate the small wins alongside the big achievements. Always provide your own celebration cakes.

Not to put a downer on anyone's mood or anything, but freelancing can be lonely! There will be days when you don't talk to anyone else. If your postman hasn't got anything for you to sign for, your chat is non-existent. This can be difficult to adjust to and it's so important that we recognise the shifts in our work rhythms and the impact they have on us. Despite what people think, freelancing comes with its own unique challenges, just like any other business. Sometimes we get to tackle these in our pyjamas, but they're still difficult.

Shifts in our mental health are often gradual and it's not always easy to see when it's happening. I spent so many months pushing down my anxiety that I didn't realise just how bad it was until I was already seriously ill. Even when I would wake up bolt upright having a panic attack. The brain excels in giving us signals that things aren't alright, but is also surprisingly good at finding ways to cope and carrying on regardless.

Self-care means something different to everyone. As much as I enjoy a bit of Diptyque, a scented candle really only goes so far. I think real self-care is about helping ourselves. Giving us a bolster cushion so we can face what's in front of us: a tough day, a tricky email, some bad news from a client. Self-care helps with our reinforcements and sometimes we need something a little tougher than an expensive candle that looks pretty on Instagram. Usually, the most basic and strongest form of self-care is free.

Resilience isn't something we should be striving for. It means we're already fighting. So prioritise what makes life easier for you: have a shower, eat a banana before you read your emails. Put boundaries in place so you aren't dealing with difficult clients at all hours (and turn to page 127 for more about that). Keep on top of the things that make you feel good to help you on the days that you don't. At least until you've filed that copy. Some days that's all we need to do.

Your home office setup

You know that old saying 'tidy desk, tidy mind'? For freelancers, 'grab a space' is more realistic. I rented homes most of my professional life. Sharing and juggling space with flatmates is hard. Between the hours of ten and six, my 'office' was usually a dining table. Then everything would pack up neatly for board games or dinner. You'll also find me working on the sofa, and – with an alarming frequency – the foot of the bed wrapped in a towel for an hour after I've got out of the shower.

While I like having a workspace, I am entirely flexible with what this means. If I'm comfortable, I can write. Your flexibility is an asset as a freelance writer. You won't always be working from home – you might be working shifts in an office, and some clients prefer you in-house, which usually means 'borrowing' a desk while Becky's on holiday. Being flexible with where you can work will help you settle in quickly while you're surrounded by someone else's wedding photos and a branded bottle of wine from the 2017 Christmas party.

In an ideal world I'd have a little writing studio at the bottom of a garden filled with roses and honeysuckle. My little tabby cat Chip would curl up next to me but stay a good foot away from my keyboard rather than trying to lie across it. I would beaver away on brilliant words all morning before stopping for a delicious lunch, probably made with tomatoes and smugness. Then I'd have a lovely afternoon of reading and drinking tea in the sunshine.

If this is your actual working-from-home life, I am supremely happy for you, and a little bit envious. It's a far stretch from the setup for most freelancers. For a start, I have little interest in growing tomatoes, only eating them. If you are lucky enough to have a dedicated space to work in, guard it with your life. Even if it's the smallest corner of a room. You'll still need to get used to constant interruptions: pets, flatmates, children, and perhaps most annoying of all, delivery drivers who have realised that you work from home (I am the parcel concierge for my entire street). Little interruptions can't be helped, so you need to get very good at either shutting things out when it's time to write, or at snatching time around everything else.

I mix and match these approaches depending on what work I've got on in my week. Sometimes I get very little writing done but I've finally put some laundry on, been to the bank, returned that dress that was a little odd around the shoulders, and called my parents. One of the greatest things about working from home is the freedom to create your own schedule. It's easy to fill an entire day with tasks that aren't actually writing, especially if you're avoiding doing something. So you need a way to get into work mode.

Some of you will slide right into it. If my laptop is within grabbing distance, I can generally just start typing away, but there are times when I need a little more help – a cup of tea, really bright lipstick (Rimmel's Furious Fuchsia) and running a brush through my hair always makes a huge difference. While I do enjoy writing in my pyjamas sometimes – as do many freelancers – they need to be clean and fresh on, rather than the ones I woke up in.

I can't tell you your own schedule or how your workday looks, and I honestly don't care what you wear when you're working. I can tell you that feeling comfortable when you work is so important. Feeling comfortable also means that you'll need a few common rules if you share a home with other people. Of course these rules get bent or broken, but if they're in place 70% of the time and I've still managed to write for forty-five minutes without interruption then I don't mind so much. Whatever your home setup is, figure out how your work life works best for you and those around you. Although we're talking about *your* career, when you're working in someone else's home, you do have to consult them before you decide that the living room is your permanent office and kick everyone out.

Ask yourself what your ideal work schedule looks like and do everything you can to make that happen. Give yourself the best chance at being able to write well. It won't always happen – there will *always* be something – but it doesn't need to derail your entire day and it's your job to fight against that happening. If you're comfortable and you've got everything you need, you're more likely to win that battle.

Exercise

1. **List five things that make you feel ready for work.**
Maybe it's breakfast, or a morning run, or having
something nice planned for dinner. Write a one-line
plan next to each item to help ensure that these things
happen as often as possible. Make a note in your diary
to try a new takeaway, block time out to exercise and
buy the good cereal.

2. **List five things you need to work your best.**
Perhaps you can't work without an incredibly hot cup
of tea or you get grumpy if you've got cold feet (these
are both me, by the way). What about background
noise? Write a line next to each one to try and ensure
your work environment is the best it can be – try
noise-cancelling headphones, buy yourself a big mug
(or a Thermos). Figure out where you need to make
changes to your current work environment.

3. **Finally, list five things that you hate interrupting
your day.** Is it calls from family? The delivery guys
who are trying to leave parcels for your neighbours?
Having to deal with a barrage of emails before you've
written a word in the morning? Make a one-line plan
for each of these (I never answer the door if I'm not
expecting a parcel). Draw boundaries around your
working hours and refer back to this list when you feel
swamped and overwhelmed.

The commandments on asking for advice

It's always flattering to be asked for advice. Whether it's a changing-room WhatsApp from a friend about a dress they're unsure of, or a pal asking how to tell a friend they've got a huge crush on them, we all like being the person called upon to solve a dilemma. When you're starting out, it's highly likely that you will seek out advice.

However, there is a right and wrong way to ask a more experienced writer or editor for advice. Especially if they're a stranger. Here are the commandments of asking a total stranger for advice. Or, to put it another way, how to be someone who is respectful of other people's time.

Thou shalt be specific.

'I'd love any advice you have!!!' Emails like this are a big part of why I wrote this book. They are impossible to reply to. Be specific about what you need help with. Otherwise, the person you're emailing is shooting in the dark. At best you'll be left disappointed with a vague response, but you may not get a reply at all.

Thou shalt ask thy question and then sit down.

Everyone rolls their eyes at the person at an event who thinks it's OK to ask five questions as soon as they grab the microphone. Do clarify if you need to, but don't reply to advice with a dozen more questions.

Thou shalt say thank you.

99% of people who ask for advice never say thank you when it's given. Don't be a dick.

Thou shalt realise that a cup of coffee is pretty flimsy.

Offering to buy someone a coffee in exchange for advice sounds nice in theory but when you throw in travel, public transport and finding your café of choice is busy so you have to go elsewhere, that coffee is now three hours out of someone's day. By all means offer to buy someone a cuppa but do acknowledge that it's a pretty flimsy offer. Don't make anyone travel for this meeting – go to them. And also, buy them cake.

Thou shalt not reply telling someone their advice is wrong.

Apparently, you don't want someone's advice, you just want someone to tell you that you're right. In almost all cases you're wrong.

Thou shalt remember you're not the only one.

If you're emailing someone asking for their advice, remember that it's highly likely that a lot of other people are, too. Bear that in mind when you start tweeting them about whether or not they saw your email (they did) and if they have had a chance to read it yet. That's none of your business and answering emails isn't anyone's job.

Thou shalt not expect – or demand – a reply.

Don't get passive aggressive, or even slightly pissy, with people for having lives outside of their inbox. We all have a finite amount of time, including you. The hour someone spends replying to emails either comes out of their writing time or elsewhere – a friend's birthday party, cooking a nice meal, reading a book. Answering one, two, three 'quick questions' means that something else has to go. It's up to the person you're emailing to decide how much time they're able to give.

Systems aren't sexy but they are smart

If you aren't a natural organiser, I understand why you might be tempted to skip straight past a section about systems and jump straight to the good stuff. Forget the spreadsheets and lists, let's get to pitching and all the fun bits of freelancing! Systems aren't sexy. But they'll help you enjoy the good bits, I promise.

A system is simply a structure that you create to help you get your work done. It might be something that helps you juggle multiple clients, or means you keep on top of your invoicing. You might put one in place to manage your side project, or to schedule your work so you can take the afternoon off on Fridays. Whether you opt for to-do lists, huge wall planners or spreadsheets, systems make your freelance life so much easier. It took me a very long time to realise this.

I didn't have a solid work foundation for the first five years of my freelance career. I muddled along and patched up the gaps whenever I needed to. Now I know that having a solid foundation will be the best thing you can do for your freelance career. The thing is, you already know this, even if you've not admitted it to yourself, but let's go all in with the metaphor anyway. Building something brick by brick only works when you've got a solid structure to begin with. It doesn't matter how nice your cushions are, your lovely freelance house is going to come crashing down around your ears the second there's a gust of wind if you don't have a decent foundation underpinning it.

Systems might not be sexy but what they allow you to achieve *is*. They help you feel secure. They make you tougher. When things start to waver around you, they don't collapse. Because of this, neither do you. A strong system and solid foundation can help you be brave. You're more likely to jump into something new when you feel like you're in control of your work, rather than sticking with the client you don't love because it's safe.

Systems give you freedom.

Now it's starting to sound a little bit sexier.

While I'm not suggesting that a to-do list can change your life, I do think how we organise our day can have a huge impact on our working week. Creating successful systems is about making things easier so you don't feel like every day's a battle. You're not failing when you have a tough day, but your systems (or lack of them) might be.

A lot of freelance joy comes from concentrating on what will make your life easier in the future, whether that's six hours or even months from now. Putting practices into place that will make your working life easier, or your Friday afternoon more fun. We can all do the hustle and slog, but every happy freelancer I know has put some time and effort into creating effective systems that help them work smarter.

I used to think that this was boring work. Now I relish it. There's nothing fancy about my systems at all. I'll crack out a colour-coded spreadsheet the second anyone suggests a new project, and I love a bullet point. They work for me. Creating effective systems is more about knowing your own weak spots than worrying about what system you use. We're just trying to solve the potential bottlenecks and help your day run smoothly. You might find yourself up against some of these problems:

- You love writing articles but you get nervous about sourcing interviews and always leave it until the last minute.
- You're always busy at the end of the week so you end up working over weekends.

- You say yes to all of the work you get offered.
- You've got 47,000 unread emails.
- You keep working well into the night even when you don't have deadlines.
- Your work is slipping because you're juggling too many things at once.
- You never have time to work on your own projects.
- You can't take a holiday, you're always too busy.

If you recognise your own work patterns in this list, you are entirely normal! All freelance writers will find they have to deal with these issues at some point. When you're juggling several projects and you don't have anyone to help you plan your workload, it's incredibly easy to feel like you're not in control of things. Effective systems make life so much easier.

Before you start getting worried that you're going to be overwhelmed by numbers and graphs and conditional formatting, consider that all of these things are effective systems that are incredibly easy to implement:

- **To-do lists.** Monthly, weekly, daily. Anything that helps you see what's on your plate. If you keep forgetting things, it can help to be super detailed and outline every part of a project. Then you also get the joy of ticking more things off. Do add 'make a cup of tea' and 'have a shower' to your list so you can cross something off immediately.
- **Weekly and monthly planners.** If you're a visual person, laying everything out in front of you can be really helpful in managing deadlines and juggling several clients' projects at once.

- **Spreadsheets.** Keep track of who you're invoicing, who you're pitching (and who you're pitching next), your article ideas, what deadlines are coming up, what projects you're working on. Anything that has moving parts probably needs a spreadsheet. The chapters for this book were outlined on a spreadsheet. They're methodical and functional and that's what you need to get the practical part of writing done.
- **Anything colour-coded (I get excited at the mere mention).** I colour-code my to-do lists in order of priority, and I change colour on my spreadsheets when I've started a job and when it's completed – I love watching everything turn the same colour.
- **Folders.** Want to keep focused? Organise your work so it's easy to find, instead of spending ten minutes searching for that one crucial piece of information. Do the same with your inbox if you keep getting lost in it, too.
- **Templates.** When you write a lot of the same emails or project proposals and rates, having an outline that you can tweak can help save you time. (You'll find an invoice template on page 221.)

You don't need to plan out every moment of your working week. Of course you can wing it. Sometimes you will. You can get by on your talent and your contacts and your brilliant work – that's why people are hiring you, after all – but we're happier when we can find the joy in our day. It's hard to find joy when you're up against it and spinning too many plates. The joy often comes after – the bubble bath with twinkly candles, the huge plate of fish and chips, the luxe face pack; it's a response to stress, but it does nothing to stop it. Good habits don't happen immediately. Like leaving your phone in another room when you go to sleep, or trying to prise the third packet of Squares from my salty fingers, it takes time.

My self-care is spreadsheets that help me plan my goals, work and cash flow, a healthy work routine and an understanding of my own weak spots so I can counteract them. When I talk about good foundations, it's to ensure you get the best out of being a freelance writer. I want you to earn money from lovely commissions and get bylines all over town, but not at the cost of your own daily happiness. Building a strong foundation and an effective way of working is the smartest way to ensure this happens.

Exercise

1. **Write a list of things that you struggle with.** Look at your recent work or comments from your editors if you're not sure. Think about how each project felt when you were in the middle of it. Your list will probably look a little like the one earlier in this section.

2. **Look for any patterns.** Do you forget to reply to emails? Do you leave your interviews to the last minute? Are you finding the admin impossible to keep on top of? Once you've acknowledged the areas that keep tripping you up, you can address them.

3. **Create a system to help you.** There's no point playing with to-do lists if you work better visually. Perhaps you need a wall planner, or you work best

with colour-coding. Good systems don't need to be sophisticated, just something that you can stick with. Pick the three most important areas and focus on those; try things for a few weeks and see how they fit.

Freelance success story
'When I first started, I wanted to write well enough that I could publish with the Guardian. That's how I defined success: getting my name into a dream publication. Then it became about financial goals: to make enough for me and my partner to live comfortably and splurge on the good stuff in life. You know: Lurpak butter and gin from an independent distillery instead of a supermarket bargain bin.

Now, it's about designing a life where my job is to get into my flow state as much and as quickly as possible, and to be able to make stuff that's genuinely worth sharing with the world. I don't know of another way of working that allows that to be your priority each day.'
Lauren Razavi, freelance writer and author of the work culture newsletter Counterflows

The last word

You can't do everything in a day.

When you're in control of the shape of your career it can feel like you're failing if you're not being productive every minute. You'll be exhausted by Tuesday afternoon if you go at it like this. Small steps make things sustainable. People tell us that we have the same number of hours in the day as Beyoncé, and while that's true, she also has an entourage bigger than most people's Christmas card list.

You are not just a freelance writer. You're running a business and you're running it solo, which means that you're also chief financial officer, HR manager, marketing manager and admin assistant. Queen Bey doesn't have to stop creating to chase her invoices.

When you concentrate on what's most important to you, the structure of your week aligns with this and you feel less stressed, less harried. Stop trying to do it all in a day, start doing the things that matter.

Getting Work

There's always one commission that makes you think, 'I want more of this'. It might be your first, or one from an editor you've always admired, but at some point you'll get a piece of work that makes the chase all seem worthwhile.

This section of the book is all about helping you get the work that you love.

Some of this work will fall straight in your lap – a boon to your confidence and finances – but most of the time you'll pitch for the work yourself. Whether you're pitching features to editors or speaking to small businesses about your skills as a copywriter, selling yourself is a vital part of being a freelance writer.

Pitching an editor you've never spoken to before requires you to be a little bit brave – sometimes it still scares me – but that bravery is often rewarded. It's also what makes a freelance writing career so brilliant. You could make a pretty good living on work that's commissioned to you directly, but if you want to shape your career – and I suspect you do since you're reading this book – then you need to hunt for that yourself. Pushing for the work that you enjoy writing more than anything allows you to take claim of the freelancing opportunities that are most rewarding for you.

That's what pitching is about. It's selling the stories that you want to tell and selling your skills so that you get to do the dream jobs. Luckily there are people who want to help make your wildest ideas, your most outlandish of pitches and most unusual stories a reality. There are editors who are itching to publish the stories that you're itching to write.

The media industry has a little bit of an 'Us vs Them' problem with freelancers and editors. We all play our part in this but when you start seeing editors as creative people who want to help you write your best work and give it a platform, pitching becomes much more enjoyable. Sure, there will be editors who dick you around, and some that you just don't work well with (and you better believe this swings both ways), but for the most part the industry is full of people who love the same things that you do and want to publish stories about the things they care about. Your job is to help them find those stories.

Pitching is a part of freelancing that you enjoy more when you focus on the stories that you can't stop thinking about, rather than the pitching ideas that you hope might stick (I've sent both this month). If you've picked up this book at a time when your writing career feels a bit wishy-washy, when you're doing work that pays alright but doesn't suit you, upping your pitching game is usually the answer. If the work you've got lined up doesn't fulfil you or make you happy, it's time to go out and get some that does.

Let's get to work.

'Where do you get your ideas from?'

The question I get asked most often from other writers, family, friends and total strangers at parties (after they've asked me how much money I earn) is 'Where do you get your ideas from?' Every writer gets asked this repeatedly, as though the answer to being a writer is just to find where the ideas are stored. There is no ideas tree. It's just hard work and listening to your instincts. This answer disappoints everyone.

You've probably tried to sit at your desk and 'come up with ideas'. Trying to think up pitches from nowhere feels unnatural, or to put it more bluntly, like punching yourself repeatedly in the face. Your words will flow eventually – you've bills to pay after all – but it's a hard way to go about things. So, let's make things a little more natural by listening to our intuition.

Your brain is constantly trying to send you writing messages. That passing thought of 'Oh, that's a good idea' or 'I wonder about...' is your signal. The wondering is what kickstarts your research. Writers are naturally curious, but that curiosity is something that we have to keep practising. It's surprisingly easy to get out of the habit.

You have ideas buzzing about all the time. They'll hit you when you're in the shower, sitting on the bus, in the middle of a conversation with a long-lost friend, in response to a piece that made you angry. All too often we ignore these ideas; we're not paying attention. We're busy with something else. We don't listen to our brain when it's shouting (sometimes whispering), 'Write this down!' and it flies by, forgotten about, possibly ready for the next writer to snap it up, if you believe in what Elizabeth Gilbert says in *Big Magic*: 'Inspiration will always try its best to work with you – but if you are not ready or available, it may indeed choose to leave you and to search for a different human collaborator.'[4]

You'll know if you've ever worked on a news desk that the ideas just have to keep coming. When you're writing five, six, seven stories in a shift, there just isn't time to sit and wonder if your idea has legs – you need to give it some.

Which brings us nicely onto the next point: your ideas are very unlikely to come at you fully formed. So many writers don't do their ideas justice because they aren't quite ideas yet. There's a nugget there, but nothing more. You need to spend time with your notes and thoughts and see if it turns into something. Not all of them will – there's a note on my phone that just says 'popsicle'. Another that says 'badgers at Christmas'. They came to nothing, although if anyone reading is keen on creating a supermarket Christmas ad about a family of badgers, drop me a line. There's also one that says 'Bernina', which turned into a lovely travel feature about my love of writing on trains. Alas, a quick filing deadline meant I had to swap the Bernina Express for a 9 a.m. train from Wrexham Central to Birmingham New Street.

The gold doesn't come ready-spun. You have to do the work, and significant chunks of it need doing before you pitch. So much of pitching is learning how to take a nugget of an idea and turn it into something that can grow – an editor can't commission a one-line pitch about 'popsicles' but a look back at how ice lollies have changed over the last 100 years? Perhaps. We'd finally get to the bottom of why the jokes on sticks vanished.

Your ideas aren't bad. When you're struggling with them, I suspect it's because they aren't developed enough. You need to hang out with them some more.

Your three-step plan for having brilliant ideas *all the time*

That's a very flashy headline for what is really – of course – another system. The point of this section is to stop you ever having to sit down at your desk and force yourself to come up with ideas. I'm all for making yourself write instead of watching Netflix, but forcing the creative process never feels great. So, it's time to set up a system that means you have good ideas waiting for you all the time.

Whatever format you use for the process, you need space for the three different pools of ideas. I tend to start in a notebook, and then when things get more detailed in parts two and three, I switch to different folders on my laptop. You might love a spreadsheet, or Trello; I prefer a good ol' Word document.

1. **Initial ideas.** Whenever your brain runs off on a tangent or starts wondering about something, write it down. Even if you don't have time to pitch anything at the moment. Add a little bit of detail but not so much that you start to second-guess yourself. The ideas that don't mean anything yet are often part of something bigger, you just haven't figured out all of the pieces.

   If this step sounds a little strange to you at the moment, think about where you usually are when you have your best ideas. I'm either in the shower or midway through a run, which means I'm either trying to type while I avoid puddles or I'm scribbling with shampoo in my hair. It doesn't matter as long as the idea gets written. Keep doing this whenever an idea strikes – it's what will keep your ideas pool full and fresh – but don't get into the habit of developing your ideas at any hour of the day as soon as they strike. You deserve your relaxation time.

2. **Development.** When you're back at your desk, start the research, follow up that train of thought. Where do you see your idea going? What needs to happen next? Is it a trip? Securing an interview? Finding a fresh angle? Is it more than one article? Explore all of the options. This is the bit where you get to have fun – it's work, but it's also noodling about on the internet and reading books or watching films. It's

51

exploration, and that's what keeps your days fun. Take your idea as far as you can.

3. **Your pitch list.** Now it's time to turn your ideas into actual pitches. Hone them and think about where you want them to go. Perhaps one idea is a travel piece, or food. Another might be suitable for tabloid, or a long-read. Determine what you are pitching and who you are pitching for. Make sure you read the rest of this chapter to polish your pitching skills.

This method means that you always have several ideas at different stages. Keep working on parts one and two; keep tinkering away on ideas even when you're not ready to pitch because you've got other work on.

You'll send some pitches immediately, but there's something lovely about seeing a call for pitches and knowing that you've got a great idea already in the works. Even if it needs more research, this approach feels organic. You can also pick and choose what you're working on with this system – reworking ideas can be easier to fit around other work than working on pitch development. Sometimes you feel like noodling around the internet and playing with that shiny new idea. All of this makes your pitching something to look forward to. When there's something in every pot, you'll never have to force yourself to sit down and think up ideas again.

How do you build contacts?

Building contacts can feel like a crucial part of the puzzle to a freelance writer. An introduction is all you need and then that editor will finally commission you, or a friend of a friend will recommend you for a gig and then BAM! A six-figure book deal lands in your lap. Things aren't so simple, but there's no denying that industry contacts can help enormously.

An introduction can turn a cold pitch into a lukewarm pitch. An editor you've met at an event may think of you for a commission. Knowing people on your beat – PRs, insiders who give great interviews – is incredibly useful to ensure you get the best stories to pitch. However, I don't think 'contacts' are what we're really looking for. We're looking for a connection; something tangible that anchors us to our industry and the work we do. That takes time and effort.

It's incredibly hard to build a freelance career on short-term wins. Editors move about, they have their own career goals and to-do lists, and not one of them has 'be a networking box for someone to tick' written on it. Don't approach your day thinking that you have to hit some arbitrary contact quota.

I can't say that there are no industry shortcuts – the problem is that those shortcuts are only open to certain people. Boris Johnson and George Osborne did not get their media positions because of their journalism skills. The industry needs to do more to address the fact that having connections matters and not everyone is given a seat at the table. I'm very aware that as far as the media is concerned, I'm in a pretty privileged position. I'm a middle-class white woman living and working in London. I fit into the industry's Freelance Writer box very nicely. I work incredibly hard, but I don't have to work nearly as hard as other writers who don't have access to the opportunities that I did. The media industry can be a closed-off place. Especially if you don't live in London. Especially if you're working class. Especially if you're a writer of colour. Especially if you have a disability. The industry talks about wanting to hear from diverse voices but that doesn't mean that everyone's moving up the bench to make room. Those voices still aren't being heard. Opportunities are still incredibly London-centric. Standing around in a bar is no fun if you don't drink. Evening events mean that writers with kids or elderly relatives to care for can't easily attend.

So here is what I know to be true: there are times when having industry contacts can be really helpful and there are times when this will feel deeply unfair when you're on the outside looking in. So let's try and break down the idea of networking so it at least feels like something everyone has a shot at.

My first job out of university was at an insurance magazine, which meant that my afternoons were spent standing in a sea of suits and pretending to laugh at jokes about underwriting, handing my business cards to red-faced men. It wasn't much fun, but hey, it was networking! It was all about making an appearance, and – the carrot dangled in front of us – getting ahead! Put me in a room with tiny food and free wine and I should be pretty happy, but the concept of networking sucks the joy out of it. I find the business-speak we use to talk about people incredibly weird. They're not acquaintances, they're 'contacts'. It sounds disingenuous because it often is.

It's ridiculous to suggest that you can only move forward in your career if you attend a central London event on a Wednesday evening, when all you can think about is sinking into a bowl of cheesy pasta. It's especially hard for freelancers to ignore the little voice in our heads: 'Go to the party! No one knows who you are! You could meet the editor who's going to give you your big break!' The fear of missing out is palpable.

So we go. None of these things happen. But we showed our face. We're getting ahead!

I am certain that no one enjoys meeting people like this. You can get good at these events (PRs are phenomenal at it; I can only watch in awe, while eating too many mini macarons), but real connections aren't easily made by throwing a bunch of strangers into a room – we learned this at school and that one time we tried speed dating. It doesn't feel natural. When we're forced to talk about work, we forget that it's the last thing any of us wants to talk about. Some people feel so negatively towards networking, a study conducted by the University of Toronto, Harvard Business School and Northwestern University concluded, that it can make us feel unclean. When recounting past professional networking experiences, the word 'dirty' came up frequently. Spontaneous networking yielded a much more positive response.[5]

What matters more than having lots of connections is what they mean to you. Having an editor tell you they loved your idea but the pitch wasn't quite right, missing out on a job but getting some great feedback and a note to keep in touch. Just a friendly chat on Twitter.

Travel writer Bethan Andrews worked in London as a magazine editor for three years until her company started trialling work-from-home days in 2017. After two years of commuting back and forth between London and Bristol, Bethan finally made the jump to freelancing full-time. 'My networking probably got a lot better because I was picking up the phone. I had PR contacts in my full-time job, but I couldn't tell you anything about them. And I'm not sure that they could tell you anything about me,' says Bethan. 'Now I feel like I've really focused on building friendships with certain PRs and editors, and building more meaningful relationships.'

Industry connections work when you bother to put the effort in. It's not all about getting commissions – don't be like the journalist who walked away at a party mid-sentence when I told them I wasn't commissioning – there is so much joy in just having a chat. You need some fun chat when you're freelance. If you're only talking to someone when they're of use to you, you're missing out on the good part of networking. Sometimes you'll discover an ally, a mate, a real friend in your industry, and those people are worth much more than a handbag full of mini macarons.

How to connect with people in the industry and still eat your cheesy pasta

Get social
If you want to get to know writers without going to events, Twitter is the best place to do it. If you're in the lifestyle/fashion/food/travel industries, head over to Instagram. There's more on page 93 about social media.

Engage in someone's work
As a group, freelance writers are very needy people. Writers like genuine compliments so if you enjoyed something they wrote, tell them.

Talk about things that have nothing to do with work
Editors like their jobs but they aren't interested in talking about their commissioning budget for an hour.

Reply to pitch rejections
Say thank you to any feedback, and actually keep in touch or follow up when you say you will.

Congratulate people on their promotions
Not just to follow up with 'Can I pitch you?' but because you're genuinely excited for your internet pal.

Thank people for sharing your work
Return the favour. Be generous.

Talk to your peers
Make new friends, engage with the conversation going on around you.

Reply to relevant press releases
'Don't just check in when you gain something from it, because I think it's so clear that that's what's happening,' advises Bethan. Thank the person who sent it to you or ask for a little more information and open up a discussion about your work and your clients.

Pitch your work
The easiest way for a writer to make connections is to talk about their work. Talk to PRs, pitch editors, share your writing on social media. Make the conversation about your ideas and put the focus on your creativity and talent.

None of these suggestions are going to immediately get you commissions but I don't think that's what networking should be about. It's about finding your place in an industry and feeling like you belong to a community. By engaging in work outside of your own – rather than thinking, 'What can this person do for me?' – you're becoming part of something bigger than your next commission. When you're a curious person and you're interested in other people, you're an interesting person to spend time with. That's what people will remember.

Working with PRs

Working with PR companies can be daunting for freelancers. It's undoubtedly easier when you're in a staff role, or when you've already got a commission from a big publication. What if you don't have that just yet but you have a great idea for a story?

As with so much of freelancing, everything comes down to research. What is it you want from a PR company? It might be product samples, a quote that goes a little deeper than the press release, or an interview or case study. You need to do a little legwork *before* you get in touch with a PR company; give them something that they can respond to and take to their client. 'I love brainstorming with freelancers. The best meetings are when we both arrive with some ideas of what can work for our clients, and what makes a good story,' says Diana Massey, director of luxury lifestyle and travel communications agency The Massey Partnership. 'Do your research, see who our clients are, and engage with us on social media, or drop us an email.'

What about all of those lovely press trips you see your peers on? They may look lush on social media, but press trips are *work*. None of your family will believe you – they'll assume you were lying on a beach for a week – but you're usually up at 7 a.m. and with the same group of people until well after midnight.

Sometimes this is brilliant fun, but it can be taxing – imagine going on holiday with your work colleagues. Every writer has a press trip horror story or five. (A journalist in Cyprus who actively and aggressively appeared to despise vegetarians; a drunk PR announcing midway through five days in Tuscany that depression was my own fault and I just needed to 'be happy'; the *Daily Mail* writer who told me right at the start of a flight to Svalbard that I wasn't a 'real woman' if I didn't have children, are some of my personal favourites.) You can't look at press trips as a holiday – it's work, and your end goal has to be the story and your bottom line. Even without a commission in your pocket, you need to know how to pitch it when you get home. Not only are press trips work, ironically they're also a week where you aren't writing, and that's not something to take lightly when you're freelance. If you get one commission worth £150, you might have spent a few days in a nice hotel, but you'll be short at the end of the month and jetlagged. It doesn't always make financial sense unless you start seeing it as an opportunity to offer unique stories to several different outlets.

When you do want in on a trip, those PR relationships come into their own. 'It's all about relationships,' says Diana. 'Most of the freelancers who have come on trips with our agency have met with us and made the effort to get to know what we're about, who we represent and how we work.'

Getting to know PRs means that they'll email with a story they know is perfect for you, or they'll share something new about a client of theirs you've covered previously. Yes, their aim is to get coverage for their clients, but they also know that the best way to do that isn't an unsolicited press release, it's through personal connections.

When you do need to contact PRs, services such as ResponseSource and Cision are great places to start. You can create a journalist request that tells PR companies exactly what you're looking for to complete your article. It might be product information, or a press trip; it could be samples or data. Your alert will go out to relevant industry representatives who can then contact you to help you with your story. You'll also find more niche offerings for certain industries – Homes4Media for interiors and property design, DIARY directory for beauty. You can also use the hashtag #journorequest on Twitter, created by journalist Sarah Ewing, which will help bring people to you on social media (this is a particularly great option when you're looking to speak to small business owners). Don't see PRs as gatekeepers or people who clog your inbox full of blanket press releases; they can be incredibly helpful and offer up stories and insight when you really need it.

Pitch, please

In its purest form, your pitch is a story. It has a beginning, a middle and an end. It talks about your article idea, but it does more than that – it talks about you and your connection to your idea, and covers the practical nuts and bolts of your article; it frames the story in a wider context. All in about 200 words. It's no wonder that pitching is the thing that trips up many freelance writers.

Your pitch isn't just selling your story, it's also selling *you*. An editor doesn't just need to know that you've got a great idea, they also need to know that their budget is in good hands and that you're going to deliver what you promised. That you've got the skills and ability to do that. When you think about this practically, it's clear why 'I'd love to interview Robert Smith!' falls apart if you can't secure that interview. A pitch is more than just a promise of some cash for you writing about what you like. It's a business transaction and you need to treat it like one.

This is why an underdeveloped pitch, two or three lines that are barely a topic outline, isn't going to get you a commission. Your prospective editor needs to know exactly what they're getting for their money. An editor can't share your idea in an editorial meeting if there's nothing there to discuss. You can't ask an art department to start mocking up those pages. You can't write it on a magazine flat-plan that tells an advertising team what they're putting their full pages next to. If you don't know what your piece is about, how can you expect someone else to know?

If you've sent a three-line pitch, know that you're not alone. I've sent them too. Editors get dozens of half-thought-out pitches every day. It doesn't mean you're a bad writer – being bad at pitching is not the same thing – but you're not giving your ideas a chance. Everyone cuts corners with their jobs sometimes, but when it comes to pitching there's no room for complacency and if this is where you're trying to save time in your work, you are doing yourself a disservice and making your job much harder. You're not in control of whether an editor commissions you, but you are in control of whether or not you send them the best pitch you can.

Why is pitching so damn hard?

Pitching is the lifeblood of most freelance writing careers. It's how you shape what kind of writer you want to be. You get to go after the clients and work that you want.

This should be exciting but for a lot of freelance writers it's also terrifying enough to stop that email being sent at all.

No matter how excited I am about pitching an article, even after years of practice, it's still a pretty nerve-wracking process. I usually make sure I've also got another job to do that takes me away from my computer immediately after pitching. Otherwise, I'm stuck in the endless email refresh.

So what is it about pitching that makes it so hard?

Fear.

Fear of rejection, fear of the unknown, fear that we're punching above our weight. The (often unfounded) fear that our ideas are terrible. We have no control around the outcome of our pitches, and despite all the elements of freelancing that I do get to have a say over, I cannot control whether an editor commissions my article or publishes my books.

No matter how excited we are by our stories, it's easy to psych ourselves out of work. There are half-written pitches in my inbox that I've been meaning to finish for weeks. I've still got brilliant pitches that got rejected and I haven't reworked them and sent them elsewhere. Sometimes we are ready to pitch new editors; other times we stick to editors and publications we're familiar with. There's nothing wrong with that. We are human, and just trying to get through the day.

Every pitch we send is something from our heads and our hearts. We pin our flag to our stories and ideas and shout 'this is good!' It's something that we believe in. So when we send that out into the world, there's a vulnerability that goes with it. Some days we knock it out of the park. Other days it's an incredibly difficult process.

It's a process that's harder when we're having trouble in other areas of our lives. When rent is late, when your period is due, when you've had an unexpected vet bill, when you've had a bad client experience. The sixth rejection in a row might be the one that sends us over the edge into sulking in front of *Dawson's Creek* and eating chips. If I'm having a tough time with my mental health, I spend that time concentrating on my own projects rather than pitching new editors. Resilience comes in ebbs and flows.

Still, pitching regularly is a part of the job and we all have to learn to dust ourselves off and try, try again. The more we pitch, the better we get at it. If we're not pitching and only waiting for offers to come to us, we're only enjoying half of what freelance writing has to offer. The opportunities we seek out and create for ourselves are the ones that can lead to the most exciting work we do. When ideas come from us, we're shaping our own potential.

That potential can stop us in our tracks. I've had my day, week, month changed by someone saying yes to an email. This book got commissioned because one person said yes to an email that I sent at 1 a.m. However, I believe that the fear that comes with pitching eases when we're pitching ideas that make our hearts happy and our brains whirr. The ideas that we have to see through because they keep us awake, they distract us, always pulling us away from whatever it is we're trying to focus on. I also think that these pitches are the ones that editors are more likely to say yes to, whatever your writing experience. Freelancing is far easier and more enjoyable when we're pitching something that we care about. So rather than concentrating on getting the commission, switch your focus so it's on the stories that you have to tell. Then you're giving yourself the tools to be brave and go after the freelance career that you really want for yourself.

Are you asking the right questions?

A common reason that editors reject pitches – or just don't reply – is that your pitch throws up the wrong sort of questions. A pitch should make an editor want to know more about your story. If your pitch isn't fully fleshed out, the questions in your editor's mind are:

So what? What's the point?
Why will my readers care?
Can this writer do this story justice?

Even if you've got a great idea, if your pitching isn't selling it – or you – you'll get a rejection. When you haven't done enough groundwork, or your pitch is wishy-washy, an editor doesn't have time to get into a huge discussion about something that's still going to come out flat.

To avoid this, you need to start asking questions that turn your pitch from something flimsy into something solid.

The story:

- What's the story about?
- What's the theme of the piece?
- Who is it about?
- Why should people care?
- Why is it important now? Do you have a news hook that makes your story relevant in a wider context?

And the logistics:

- What style of piece are you writing?
- Which section of the publication does it sit in?

- Do you have interview access if you need it? Photos? Recipes?
- Can you turn this piece around quickly if you need to?
- Is it an exclusive?

If you can answer every single one of these questions concisely and you really believe in your pitch, it's ready. If you're uncertain about any of these points, find out the answers before you hit send. Don't hope an editor will fill in the blanks. Make it easy for an editor to be shouting 'YES! This is the pitch I have to commission today!'

Do you have a news hook?

Pegging your stories to something in the news gives an editor a reason to publish your piece. Some publications insist on it, but even if one doesn't, it's a good habit to get into – it elevates your pitches considerably. Studies and surveys are a great way of doing this without feeling the need to 'comment on the news'. Birthdays and anniversaries are helpful, too – mark these on your calendar twice: the actual date of the event, and the date that you should start pitching around these topics so you don't miss the boat, just as you would around Christmas. If you're pitching magazines with particularly long lead times, a direct news hook will be outdated, but your stories do need to connect to a wider cultural discussion. Some freelance writers struggle with this but when editors are asking you 'why now?' or telling you that your pitch is interesting but it's not the right time, you need to work a little harder at nailing that news peg. When you get this right, it helps your stories feel part of a bigger conversation.

Switching your pitching mindset

There was a point in pitching when I realised that I felt like I was walking up to editors with a bowl and begging them for words. It's not cool to admit it, but I was desperate for someone, anyone to say yes. I had lost control of my pitching. I started pitching pieces that I thought an editor would say yes to, not the pieces that I wanted to be writing. It took me a long time to realise where I was going wrong.

You are the only person who can write your stories. With your style, your angle, your wit, your sources. If you're doing it right, what you're selling is unique and you're giving an editor the opportunity to buy that.

If gratitude is what you feel every time you get a commission, it's time to switch your mindset. You're offering an editor the chance to publish a brilliant story that they wouldn't get to otherwise. If they don't jump at that opportunity for whatever reason, you get to take it elsewhere because it's still a brilliant idea. The book industry does this so well. Agents shout about a pitch they love like it's the greatest piece of work since *Wolf Hall*. That's the confidence we need to bring to our pitching! Present your ideas as an opportunity because you're excited to work with an editor and think their publication is the best place for your article and you're offering it to them first. When you hold your head high while you're pitching, your approach changes. Not only does your story outline get better, but your confidence often means that you get a response even if it's a no. You start building those relationships, even if the pitch isn't quite right for that editor.

If you believe in your stories, believe that they should be on the pages of a magazine because you're a damn good writer, then you need to pitch them in a way that sells it. Make editors believe in what you're selling, because what you're selling is brilliant.

> **Exercise**
>
> **Give your old pitches a news hook.** Go through your recent rejected pitches and give them a solid news hook. Look for current studies that will help you, or consider how a change in news can help bring life to an old pitch. Rework those pitches and send them out again with a fresh lick of paint.

Things that are not a pitch

Dear Sir/Madam,

I really like your magazine. Are you accepting pitches at the moment?

Thanks,
Writer for hire

***

@editoratmagazine
Looking for pitches from freelance writers! All topics considered, pay rate is depressingly in alignment with the rest of the industry. Email in bio!

@writerforhire
Hi @editoratmagazine I'm interested! Please email me more deets!

***

Hi Sian,

Love your site, I want to write about pizza for you!

Thanks,
Writer for hire

Your pitch should always tell a story. It needs to be something that an editor can get excited about. You may have some instances where an editor contacts you with a specific commission, but they don't do that with writers that they don't know. All your one-line email about pizza tells them is that you aren't willing to put the work in. Don't go down this route, it's a waste of everyone's time. You're unlikely to even get a reply. Make sure you serve up some real ideas.

The biggest pitching myths

To many freelance writers, pitching still feels like something mystical. There is no magic spell, unfortunately, but there are some myths around pitching that put fear into writers so much that it's enough to stop them pitching completely.

Myth: my editor is laughing about my pitch at their desk
Honestly, no one has time for this.

Myth: your editor rejected your pitch, they'll never commission you again

In almost all cases, editors reject ideas, not writers. And ideas and pitches can always be improved upon. 'Keep pitching!' says a former *WIRED* editor Vicki Turk. 'If I don't commission a few of your pitches, it's nothing personal – and I genuinely do really want you to pitch again.' Editors only ever say this when they want to hear more from you.

Myth: editors only commission published writers

It is easier to get commissioned when you've got the clips to back it up, which is something of a paradox, but editors are always looking for a fresh voice.

Myth: you made a typo, you can kiss your commission goodbye

In an ideal world you'd have never made that typo and your pitch would have been word perfect. If an editor is excited by your pitch that won't be reason enough not to commission you. They won't overlook seven errors in five lines.

Myth: there's a perfect time for pitching

Some editors read pitches when they have time, others commission daily and prefer pitches to land before 9 a.m. – there's no doubt that the early bird catches the worm when it comes to opinion pieces. Some have a monthly editorial meeting and only go through pitches a couple of days before. Some pieces might be more time sensitive, so all of the usual rules go out of the window. The only way to find out is by pitching and getting to know editors. But you can be certain that no one is going to reject a pitch *because* it landed on Friday afternoon or at 3 a.m. on a Thursday.

The ten most basic pitching errors

1. Getting someone's name wrong. Or calling them sir/madam. Put some effort in.
2. Not following pitching guidelines on the publication website or ignoring what an editor asked for in their pitch call.
3. Cutting and pasting your pitch and keeping the reference to the previous publication in your email.
4. Pitching an idea, not a story.
5. Pitching a piece that has just been published by the website.
6. Pitching a piece that the magazine would never cover.
7. Pitching a story that the magazine covers every week in a regular column.
8. Asking what sort of pitches an editor would like. Just pitch!
9. Pitching your idea to another editor on the same desk when an editor rejects your pitch.
10. Not reading the publication. Not reading the publication. Not reading the publication.

I have done literally all of the things on this list.

Pitching advice from editors

What are editors really looking for from a pitch? Here's some brilliant advice from a few of them:

Figure out where your piece would go. Don't just think about whether the topic is right for the publication – think about whether the structure or format of the piece you want to pitch is suitable. *Lucy Douglas, former* **Positive News** *editor*

I can't count the number of pitches I've received which bear little resemblance to any of the features slots or franchises I commission for. It shows a writer hasn't read your magazine or website and isn't familiar with what you do. I see a lot of good ideas that, as a consumer, I'd love to read, but they don't correspond to anything I commission as an editor. When you tailor pitches, it shows you're familiar with the brand. *Cyan Turan,* **Cosmopolitan**

Ask yourself this: does my pitch solve a problem for who I'm pitching to? Is it something new for them, something different? *Simon Brew,* **Film Stories**

Lead with a headline. Even if it's not the one that ends up on the page, it demonstrates you've thought about the hook for your piece and will help harried editors visualise it quickly. *Sam Parker,* **Penguin.co.uk**

Mention another article you've seen in the magazine that you think makes a good model for your piece. This shows you've read the magazine – flattery always helps – and it's a good prompt for us in envisaging the feature. *Frances Ambler,* **The Simple Things**

A contributor to *Pit* had clearly mapped out her idea very well before sending it over to me. She had included a paragraph in the pitch that I later saw in the piece. So she hadn't just typed out a rough idea but taken the time to craft a paragraph so good it went into the final copy. That level of quality sticks out immediately. *Helen Graves,* **Pit**

Editors don't expect you to know every article they've published but do spend some time scrolling through the last few months' articles to check your idea hasn't already been written. And if it has, all is not lost and you can still pitch something else. *Paisley Gilmour, former* **Cosmopolitan** *sex and relationships editor*

A really good pitch will give me a clear understanding of what the facts of the story are, but also a sense of the writer's style. *Vicki Turk, former editor at* **WIRED**

What can inexperienced writers do without samples?

There's a real catch-22 in the creative industries. You need experience to get ahead, but you can't get experience without someone giving you a shot... which is much harder when you don't have experience. So when you're a fledgling freelance writer, how do you deal with the issue of clips and writing samples?

Think less about the clips you don't have and focus on the ones that you do. 'Don't worry if you don't have relevant published work – I would be happy to read a blog post or unpublished piece of work if it shows that you're ideal for the publication. I would rather read that than a mass of irrelevant clips,' says writer and deputy editor of *The Simple Things* lifestyle magazine Frances Ambler. Editors won't read through dozens of clips. They'll read one or two and that should be enough to get a sense of your work. Relevant clips are far, far more important.

Of course, this in itself can still pose a problem – you still need to get those writing samples to be in with a shot. This is when writing for your university newspaper can help you and writing your own newsletter or blog posts can be a foot in the door. Showing knowledge and interest in your topic is vital, and writing samples might not be the only way that you can do that. If you're pitching a news piece about a local community issue and you've been volunteering at your local food bank, this personal experience supports your pitch even if your writing samples are about something different. 'Take extra care to lay out your feature idea – your angle, who you will speak to and why – so you show you know what you're doing,' says Frances. Well-crafted pitches are so important to freelance writers, but this is especially true when you're just starting out. When your samples are sparse, an editor is going by what's in those short paragraphs, so you need to make them the absolute best they can be. This isn't the place to cut corners – an editor is unlikely to follow up if you do. Make sure you know your story inside out. The best way to get more samples is to stop worrying about not having many notches on your desk and working the hardest you can to get some.

Your portfolio might get you attention from editors, especially if you're sharing your pieces on social media and working on building a reputation for your work, but writing samples aren't what will get you a commission. They play a brilliant supporting role and back up your pitch, but the story is still the leading lady in your matinee production of *Sally and the Fabulous Freelance Commission*. Editors will pay for your story and your unique angle if they believe that it's worth commissioning. There are some editors and publications who love working with new writers and honing that talent. Every editor in the industry was once a writer without any clips. 'A fantastic pitch can make up for a lack of experience – I'll take a gamble on a new writer if I really want the story,' says Vicki Turk.

Once again, we come back to telling the stories that only you can tell, with an angle that only you can write. This is where you hone your skills as a new writer. And once again, this is where you'll find the work that you enjoy the most.

I'm aware that this is a rather rose-tinted way of viewing the media industry. Not every publication is welcoming new writers with open arms. Unfortunately, not every editor has the time to dedicate to this process. Editing copy from a new writer can be much more labour-intensive than working with a writer who has been around the block a few times (compare your very early writing with your work now and you'll see so much improvement). It's incredibly hard not to take this personally, but there are only so many hours in a day and most editors are overworked and dealing with a shoestring budget that someone keeps trying to cut. While getting a commission should always be about the pitch and the talent, sometimes that's not the case; sometimes commissions happen because an editor needs good copy and they need it fast.

So what's the solution here? Being realistic about what you're pitching can help. It is unlikely – though absolutely not impossible – that an inexperienced writer with no clips will get a cover story. Your first commission out of the gate probably isn't going to be a 5,000-word interview with your favourite rock band. And if you're pitching that story, ask yourself exactly what you can do better than the music editor of the publication. Why should you do that interview? Pitch for work you know that you can do well, so when you deliver it – on time, to brief – your editor is eager to commission you again. You might be inexperienced but your reputation and work ethic speaks volumes.

While I'm all about reaching for the big goals, smaller publications can be such a huge asset when you're starting out. That doesn't necessarily mean taking on unpaid work (there's more about that on page 169). Many smaller publications have commissioning budgets, often factored in before an editor makes a penny, and they're small teams that work tightly with their freelance writers. Smaller publications tend to have smaller budgets so often commission fewer pieces, but you are far more likely to get helpful and honest feedback. That detail can make all the difference in the early stages of your career.

You should also think about how you're selling yourself. If you're apologetic about the fact you've just graduated, or you keep telling editors that you're an 'aspiring' writer, it's much harder for an editor to put their faith in you. You might be nervous, but save that for your WhatsApp group – let your work stand on its own, without undermining it at every turn. Don't tell an editor that you don't have many clips, or apologise for the ones that you're sharing – all you're doing is pulling attention away from the reasons someone should commission you. Shine a light on what you're good at, put the focus back on your story and your skill as a journalist.

The pitching process can be difficult but the stone-cold truth is that editors *want* you to succeed. They want to commission a brilliant piece from an unheard voice and fill the pages of their publication with a story that will resonate with their readers. Some editors will be more approachable than others, some publications will be easier to crack than others, but no one is trying to trip you up. When you get a commission it's because an editor believes in your work and the story. And in you.

What a successful pitch looks like

Here are some examples of winning pitches from freelance writers – all of these went on to be commissioned and published.

> *Norfolk's Deep History Coast – new 25-mile coastal trail*
> *Stonehenge? Pah. The North Norfolk coast claims to have the earliest evidence of mankind outside of the Great Rift Valley, and a new twenty-five-mile cliff trail, from Weybourne to Cart Gap, focuses on the area's prehistory (as well as taking in several gusty seaside towns). There are eleven 'Discovery Points' en route, triggered by an app, showing how the area would have looked in the past. The final Discovery Point is being put in place in October, but the rest of the trail can be completed already. I'd aim to visit in September, to show the benefits of heading to the area when the summer crowds have gone.*
>
> *As well as offering belting coastal scenery, highlights include Happisburgh, where footprints dating back 800,000 years have been found, and West Runton, where the UK's biggest mammoth skeleton was unearthed (part of it is on display en route).*

This pitch by award-winning travel writer and children's book author Ben Lerwill was for a national newspaper. 'I'd been in touch with the relevant editor a few days earlier and knew she was open to UK ideas. The resulting research trip was fascinating, and a good lesson in treating each commission as an opportunity in its own right: I've since written about the trail for a couple of other publications, and have written a children's book on the Stone Age. It's sometimes very easy to treat features as one-off pieces of work, but it can be really valuable to view them as springboards for further ideas and opportunities.'

***

I tried making phone calls every time I needed to talk to someone – for a week

As a millennial and an introvert, I don't often use my phone for its primary intended purpose: the phone call. I obviously do not have a landline. I do not answer phone calls with no caller ID, my phone is always on silent and my voicemail message says, 'You'd be better off texting me.' How much am I missing out on this traditional form of communication? Is my life somehow emptier for the absence of a human voice at the end of the line? Would I find confidence in chit-chat and human interaction if I called people? To find out, I propose an experiment: I call people for a week. My friends, my interview subjects, my parents, my sister, my electricity company. Anything I'd usually do by text or email, I'll do by phone. I'll answer all phone calls, too. Let's see how that goes down and if I can overcome the enormous surge of fear in my tummy every time my phone rings. Please understand this will be genuine suffering for my art.

This pitch by Kate Leaver led to a commission at British *Vogue*. 'I sent three pitches in one email, I'd only just started working with [my editor] at *Vogue* (I noticed they were publishing a few non-fashion-related features and took a shot) and she commissioned two out of three, which was wonderful. I often go for a three-pitch email when I'm new to a particular editor because I feel like I can give them an idea of the range I cover, even if they don't pick up every idea.'

***

Would love to write something about lap cheong *(Chinese preserved wind-dried sausage). It's a classic Chinese ingredient where you can find it in many dishes such as claypot rice,* lo mai gai *(glutinous rice lotus leaf wrap), congee and dim sum, etc. I think some of the best ones are handmade in Sheung Wan in Hong Kong but in the UK Poon's has been making their own since 1973 and you can buy them in Asian supermarkets like SeeWoo, Wing Yip and Hoo Hing. For this piece, I'd love to find out the process of making the sausage, what makes for a good sausage, why does it need to be hung out to dry and learn about Poon's rich history. Also, covering the different kinds and varieties of wind-dried sausages ranging from those made using fresh pork to those made using pig livers, duck livers and even turkey livers, and how each Asian region differs.*

Angela Hui was commissioned to write this piece for food magazine *Pit*. 'I emailed prior asking about rates before going ahead pitching. I think one piece of advice for pitching in any field would be to be upfront about fees and payment before sending anything over. I knew a fair bit about *lap cheong* (Chinese sausages) as I grew up eating them religiously and my parents would smuggle them back in suitcases from Hong Kong whenever we went back to see family.'

***

In the tropical world of drop shipping, you can monetise your side hustle and live the dream – or lose big

Drop shipping is when people buy items from China's AliExpress website, market them in the West for much higher prices, and then have them sent directly to consumers – most of the time without ever seeing the product they're selling. It's all made possible by Shopify, which allows the retailers to rebrand products as their own and manage orders.

Once you know what drop shipping is, you can see it almost anywhere you choose to look for it. Depop is full of drop-shipped replicas of popular dresses from brands like Reformation or Réalisation Par – you buy the imitation at less than a tenth of the price of the original, wait weeks, and are typically sent a low-quality product which bears no resemblance to the image being used to market it. Drop shippers find a product that is popular in the West – copper storage baskets, faux-marble planters, eco-friendly bamboo toothbrushes – and market it, typically via Facebook, using sponsored ads.

There are two global drop-shipping hubs: Chiang Mai in Thailand, and Canggu, in Bali. Visit these towns, and you'll find they're full of people throwing around phrases like 'passive income' whilst tapping at MacBooks in one of the city's many coworking cafés. (Ask many of these entrepreneurs what they do, and they'll say they work in e-commerce, because a stigma persists around drop shipping.)

For every entrepreneur making easy money through drop shipping – and there are some – there are even more people who travel to these tropical locations with dreams of making it big and escaping the grind, and end up losing all their savings. Because if it's easy to make money via drop shipping, it's arguably easier to lose it. There are horror stories of people losing huge sums of money, or sending thousands of pounds' worth of faulty products to the USA. I spoke with one young entrepreneur who set up a drop-shipping business selling eco-friendly homeware to socially conscious Americans – only to find, to her horror, that everything was arriving wrapped in layers of plastic, weeks late, from her Chinese factory.

There's a dark side to it all: in addition to potentially losing huge sums of money, the drop-shipping world is replete with scam artists. These drop-shipping gurus promise they can teach you the secrets of drop shipping by attending webinars, purchasing e-books, or even going to residential courses. People are sold a lifestyle: you move to Bali, make loads of money, hang out with other digital nomads, and monetise your side hustle even further by selling PDFs explaining how people can do the same. Rumour has it, they're mostly making their money not from actual drop shipping, but from marketing themselves as drop-ship gurus.

In actual fact, the Facebook algorithm changes so fast it's relatively hard to know what will sell – one drop shipper tells me that 'Facebook today is different to Facebook last year', which makes it easy for people to lose money. And Instagram influencers have also increasingly got in on the scam. Makeup YouTubers Tana Mongeau *and Gabbie Hanna were recently criticised for selling low-quality makeup brush kits that were poor-quality drop-shipped products from China.*

I'd like to write a feature looking at the world of drop shipping – the people making a killing from it, and the people who are losing all their money (you need around 5k to start doing it properly) – as well as looking at the dark side of what drop shipping represents. Who are the people in China making these low-quality products so that Western entrepreneurs can escape the grind and live their digital nomad dreams out on a beach? What is the human cost to them? What does drop shipping represent about late-capitalist entrepreneur culture? And is it really possible to create a profitable industry out of your side hustle?

Sirin Kale's pitch has a lot more detail in it than the previous examples. Her long read was commissioned by *WIRED*, and it's a great example of the detail you should be looking to include when you're pitching an in-depth feature.

How to deal with rejection

Rejection is undoubtedly one of the hardest parts of being a freelance writer. It makes us question ourselves, it dents our confidence, and if we've had one knock too many that can have a serious impact on our mental health and confidence.

Having to deal with rejection will happen at any point in your career, at any time of the day. I've learned not to check my emails in restaurants when a client has gone for a wee – last time I did that I had about thirty seconds to pull myself together after a book project got the thumbs down. Nothing pisses on your day more than rejections for breakfast – let yourself have a cup of tea before you open up your email.

There's an assumption that after you've been freelancing for a while, you never have to deal with rejection and everyone says yes to every idea you ever have. It's just not the case. Veteran freelancers might see a few more direct commissions land in their inboxes, but social media doesn't ever show us the whole picture. We don't see the hard work or the number of times a piece was pitched before it was published – even the editor who eventually commissions the writer doesn't know that.

The finished piece is never the whole story.

We know this. Of course we do. We know it from our own work, our own pitches and our experiences. So why don't we listen when the rejection email pops into our inbox? What is it that makes us take rejection so personally?

Actually, our brains are wired to be hurt by rejection. Studies have found that there's a real connection between physical pain and social rejection – the same area of our brain is activated in both situations.[6] Evolutionary psychologists believe this stems from when humans couldn't survive on their own. Social rejection was, in effect, a death sentence. That physical pain was a warning. Things aren't so extreme these days – you won't die if an editor doesn't go for your *Mario Kart* pitch – but there's a certain reassurance in the science behind why it stings so much. We still thrive on social acceptance, and that hurt you feel is very real.

When someone turns down our pitch, I think a lot of the disappointment comes from the *potential* of a project or commission. Writers and creatives are dreamers, and we know the influence that our body of work has on the shape of our future career. We are gunning for that cover story. We really hope to get that commission for that publication we love. We can spend a lot of time thinking about the domino effect of a commission. That can be financial, too – it's hard not to mentally pay my electricity bill with a commission that I don't even have yet. Freelancing is often about letting ourselves get our hopes up and while I really think this can be a good thing, it also means we're setting ourselves up for a bit of a fall when rejection comes knocking at our door.

We're often told that we shouldn't take rejection personally, but writing *is* personal. Freelancing is personal. We are our businesses. When you pour so much of yourself into a pitch, that is personal. Of course it is. You care about your pitches, you put your heart into your research. You might even put a piece of your story or your own trauma into it. Of course that's personal.

However, the reason your pitch was rejected almost certainly isn't personal.

Reasons for rejection are so varied. Perhaps it's budget, your pitch might be similar to another just commissioned, your pitch might have been a little flat, or your editor might just not be that keen on it. You can guess as much as you like, but the answer is very, very rarely an editor deciding to take a dislike to you. I've been commissioned by editors who don't like me very much; they care more about the story.

While the reason might not be a personal one, it might be something that you can do something about. It is worth pricking your ears up to feedback, and asking for it if you've pitched a couple of times but feel like you're hitting a wall and you're not sure why. If you keep getting told your timing is off, schedule notes on your calendar for certain editors and the best times for the publications. Make a note of important dates and anniversaries well in advance. If you're often told your news hooks aren't strong enough, use this to pitch better. Don't write the editor off or decide they're wrong. They're doing what's best for the publication. Listen to what they're telling you.

If you don't get any feedback then you're left with something trickier – having to deal with the emotional side of rejection without being able to fix it with practical measures. And that's hard. The best way to approach this is by having faith in the story you're pitching. When I am 100% into a story and absolutely must tell it, I work my hardest to find it a home. I don't just pitch to one place, I keep banging on doors. Rejection is still part of the process but it's far easier to deal with when I believe in what I'm doing. It's why I spoke to five literary agents about this book.

Even when we try not to let it, rejection causes our faith in ourselves to waver. It's easy for us to lose steam in an idea when one, two, three, maybe even ten editors have turned it down. But when you are backing your work and your research, you're backing yourself.

I've lost count of the number of pitches that I should have pitched elsewhere after they got rejected. There are countless ideas I didn't give enough of a push to and stories that I decided not to tell because one person I've never met said no. Sometimes dealing with rejection means pushing through it, stubbornly. Do everything you can so your pitches can become stories. You'll love the work a lot more when you don't give up on it at the first hurdle.

Exercise (desk treats are strongly encouraged)

Take a recently rejected pitch and properly examine it. Ask a friend to help you with this if you need to. Where are the weak points? Where could you have made something clearer? If an editor has given feedback, look at how you can keep the heart of your story but improve the way you're telling it. Add case studies and sources, be more specific. When you've tweaked and polished again, pitch it elsewhere. Then move on to another pitch. While you're on a roll, go onto the next. The more rejected pitches you can find homes for, the easier you're making your job.

When your resilience is low

Some rejections fly off me. I don't notice them because I'm busy working on other commissions or I've just had some brilliant news. Things are good, I'm not counting the pennies. I love the days I'm not gripping so tightly to my pitches. (I'm telling you now, days like this are when you should complete your tax return.)

Then there are the days when a rejection can break you.

I've had rejections that have hurt enough to send me back to work full-time. Once I decided to leave the media industry entirely and I was so serious about it that I applied for a job in Thailand. Leaving the actual continent seemed preferable to sending out even one more pitch.

There is a flaw in our pitching system. It is overwhelmingly time-consuming for editors and freelance writers. Most of us are stabbing in the dark and hoping for the best result. There is a huge amount of work involved on both sides of an email – research and honing on our side, feedback and sifting through inboxes on an editor's side – and no one seems to be winning from it. Editors are beginning to understand that the odds are stacked against freelancers. They're doing their best to help writers get a foot in the door, to make the process easier and to be honest about the best way to pitch them. It's different for every editor, and just when we feel we've got it right, we realise that our pitching methods don't work when we go knocking at another door.

Every pitch rejection chips away at our resilience, a dent in our battle armour. One chink might be fine, but after a few knocks we're not going to find it as easy to get back up. And after a while, if we don't repair our armour then we're going to find ourselves wiped out on our backsides with the last push. So let's talk a little bit about how to keep your resilience strong, how to repair your armour and how to keep going.

Ask for testimonials
Email clients and editors who love working with you and ask them for a few words to share on your website. Keep a 'nice comments' folder and every time someone says something nice about your writing (or your hair), squirrel it away. Read the comments when you're having a rough day and you'll be beaming.

Reread work you're proud of
Sure you've had some tough knocks recently, but you've done brilliant work before. It'll happen again.

Ask your peers about your work
WhatsApp your best people and fish for compliments. Ask your pals what they like about your writing. You'll be surprised and

delighted by the answers and it will give you a fresh perspective on your talent.

Edit your CV

No, I know, don't fall asleep. Your CV is a concise list of everything you've achieved professionally in the last two to three years. There's no space for modesty here. Spend a couple of hours bigging yourself up.

Take a break

I am all for pushing through a rough patch but sometimes we need to practise gentleness. If you need a break from things – pitching, the internet, everyone else in the whole world announcing book deals on Twitter – then take a step back. Sometimes resilience is about protecting ourselves, and the best way to do that is with a blanket and a pile of hash browns. You aren't failing by giving yourself time to recover from something that's actually pretty brutal. You're building yourself up again. That kindness gives you the power to come back fighting stronger.

How to deal with radio silence

Radio silence can be worse than a flat-out rejection. The waiting and wondering are the hardest parts of freelancing, and it can be difficult not to take dozens of unanswered emails personally, especially when you think you've written a winning pitch. Try and remember that editors are spinning a dozen plates at any one time, and some are getting hundreds of pitches every week. Like you, they're just getting on with their job. It is impossible to reply to everyone – you know this from the number of times you don't call your parents back or leave a friend on read. Still, sometimes you have a niggling voice that your pitches are being ignored.

'Much of it is down to luck,' says former *Positive News* editor Lucy Douglas. 'There are so many reasons why a pitch might get turned down or ignored, even if the pitch itself is brilliant. That sounds disheartening but the one way to guarantee you *don't* get a commission is to not send the pitch.'

When should you follow up?

I'm sure I've lost out on commissions because I was too scared to send a follow-up email. Surely if an editor didn't reply it's because they hated the pitch, so why would we even remind them about it? It's so easy to psych ourselves out, but it just isn't true. Deep down I know this from the times I *have* followed up and that's led to a commission. There are dozens of reasons you didn't get a reply. Every editor is different, and the more you get to know them the easier it becomes to judge your timing – I have an uncanny ability to email the same moment an editor turns on their out-of-office and goes on holiday for two weeks. By lunchtime your email isn't even on page two of an editor's inbox. Commissioning might be part of an editor's job but answering emails isn't. Be patient and polite.

If your pitch is particularly time sensitive, mention this in the subject line. (Note, the time-sensitive nature around the pitch is not that you fancy going out for an ice cream.) Otherwise, there's a simple follow-up rule of thumb: a polite chase after a week, then again three days later letting the editor know that if you don't hear back by end of play, you'll take the pitch elsewhere.

Is it all a numbers game?

There's a lot of talk about sending pitches being a bit of a numbers game. You might have read about aiming for a certain number of pitches in a month, or shooting for 100 rejections in a year – a concept that was suggested by literary publication Lit Hub back in 2016 as a practice for short stories and creative writing, not pitching features and articles.[7] While there's something in the idea that the more you pitch, the more success you'll have, it's not as simple as firing ideas all over the place.

Pitching frequently encourages you to try new ideas and approach new editors. You hone your technique, you get braver. You stop limiting yourself or second-guessing your ideas. You open new doors and discover new potential outlets for your writing. You're doing the research, you're putting the work in. *This* is why you're getting more commissions.

If you're unsure about your pitching technique, firing ideas off left, right and centre isn't going to get you the results that you're hoping for. It's possible that you'll end up feeling less excited by the ideas you're sending out. If you're not enthusiastic about your pitches, there's no reason that an editor should be either. Even if you do get the commissions, remember that you actually have to do the work – the best thing you can do for yourself is pitch stories that your heart is in! If you're scattergun pitching, you could end up with half a dozen features on your to-do list but only care about one. You might be glad of the money and pleased with the bylines, but you're still setting yourself up for a few weeks of dragging your feet and not engaging positively with your work.

Rather than plucking an arbitrary number out of the air, think about the end result. Do you need more articles to write, or are you hoping for commissions from certain publications? Do you want to be getting paid more money? Aim for something specific rather than throwing mud at the wall and seeing if it sticks. 'Think about the future,' says freelance travel writer Lottie Gross. 'Don't just think about now. Will the work really help you in the future, in two years' time? Will it bolster your career?' When we think about this, we come back to our 'why', our own definition of success. That adds up to much more than a numbers game.

Freelance success story

'I used to think I'd feel like a success when I got more print commissions, or when I got a book deal, or when I won an award, but then you reach those milestones and you're already beating yourself up for some other perceived failure – the print commission was edited into oblivion, the book hasn't sold well enough, someone else won a bigger award...

These days I try to keep my benchmark for success as: paying the bills, getting nice feedback from people who've read my stuff, and shutting my laptop at 6 p.m. most days. Other people might find satisfaction in working like a dog but personally I'd always rather be less 'successful' and spend more time watching telly.' **Lauren Bravo, fashion writer and author of How to Break Up with Fast Fashion**

Exercise

1. **Follow up.** Follow up on every single pitch you've sent in the last three weeks. Go for a walk after this, and leave your phone at home so you stop refreshing your inbox.

2. **Rework your pitches.** If you get a rejection after following up, rework those pitches and send them to another publication.

3. **Follow up again.** After three days, give an editor a final nudge. Then either work on your lovely commissions, or repeat step two.

The long and short of it

When the force that's driving you is positive, I am all for regular pitching. It's easy to get out of the habit when you've got regular work ticking along, or to feel like you've lost the skill after you've been working on a big piece – my pitching was as rusty as a bag of old nails after finishing this book. Like starting a car that hasn't been driven for a while, it can take some a while to get things going.

When I was pitching early on in my career, I was all about the story and not necessarily the execution of the piece. This was enough to get me commissions but I left it to an editor to tell me how long my piece was, rather than fully crafting it in my own mind first. This is the lucky dip of commissioning. You win a prize, but you have no idea what you're going to get. You're not shaping how much you get paid, or your workload. It's like asking someone else to cut you a slice of cake and getting half the amount you were hoping for.

Now I know exactly what I'm pitching for before I send that email. A quick 400 words, an 800-word piece, something more in-depth that will take a few weeks. I know how much work I could potentially have on my plate at any one time. I can tell if I'm going to be able to juggle everything with the work I've already committed to, or around holidays and events I've got coming up. There's no point pitching a detailed feature just before you go on a press trip for a week.

If you're a little relieved when an editor rejects your pitch because you have no idea how you'd fit it in, it's time to reconsider your approach. There are some cases when an editor will tell you exactly how many words they need, and that's the space they've got and you can take it or leave it, but if you've got it into your mind that your piece is a huge photo essay across ten pages and an editor offers you 400 words, you're not going to feel great about that commission. If you go some way to shaping the article in your pitch, you're far more likely to get the piece you were hoping for. This approach makes your pitch stronger – you're helping an editor visualise where your piece fits in their magazine. Just as you can find yourself being paid less for your idea than you had anticipated, things can work the other way. If an editor asks for 5,000 words when you've only got the capacity in your week to write a shorter piece, you'll be left in a difficult position. Even if you can take on the work, having longer lead times and deadlines means you've got to wait even longer to get paid and that can be the last thing you need.

Juggling short-term and long-term pieces helps keep your cash flow steady. It can do the same for your mental health, too. If you're writing a lot of personal pieces, you need something to break up the emotional demand. It's about the ebb and flow of your workday. We can't always go hard at it every single day; we need time to research, time to sit with our ideas and properly think about them. Give your work the space it needs and get smart about shaping how your week looks. The story should always come first but the long and short approach to pitching gives you some breathing space, which gives you the opportunity to create your best work.

Exercise

Examine a previously rejected pitch. Is it for a short piece or a long feature? Can you tell? Could it be two short pieces across different industries? Edit the pitch so it's suitable for a shorter article, and then a longer one. Now decide which you prefer – and which you have the capacity to write – and pitch it.

Using social media as a freelancer

My writing career grew with social media. Twitter wasn't a big thing when I went freelance. It wasn't something that you needed a strategy for. No one was being cancelled, the main order of the day was fun rather than anger and hot takes. Not to be all 'when this was nothing but fields', but I miss the time when I could tweet to see if anyone was around for a drink and an hour later, I'd be in The Grapes in Limehouse with a pint and my favourite people.

It's a lot harder to get your head around social media now, when it feels like it's nothing but a tool for self-promotion or a space where women are hounded for writing something that men don't like. Our idea of influence has shifted, too. It can feel like having a huge following on social media equals a dreamy writing career. The opposite is true: my writing is what made my social media following grow.

Although it has its issues, social media – particularly Twitter – is usually fun for me. I use it for work, sure, but I also enjoy it – I met half of my bridal party on Twitter. People forget when they start using social media in any sort of professional capacity that it can be just chats about kittens and what you had for dinner (I will always want to know what you are cooking). We spend so much time in offices talking about topics that aren't at all related to work and it keeps us going. There's lightness on social media, if you look for it, as well as an opportunity to find work. Without that lightness, Twitter's refusal to do anything about the abuse and trolls gets heavy quickly.

Twitter can be a real ice-breaker with editors. It doesn't feel like cold pitching when you're emailing someone you chat to regularly – they'll be pleased to see your name pop up in their inbox. Similarly, you're more likely to be in the forefront of someone's mind for a piece if they've just had a Twitter conversation with you about the same topic. If you talk a lot about a particular topic on social media, you're already carving out a niche for yourself (for more on that turn to page 143). It's cliquey, but it's still true that freelance work gets discussed in DMs; pitches and commissions are made in those little windows on our phones.

You don't have to use social media to do your job as a freelance writer. Plenty managed before Twitter appeared in our lives, and there are so many writers who rarely pop up at all. But you should consider the role that social media plays in the publications that you want to write for, and be aware of the role it can play in getting you writing work. Editors sometimes like writers to have at least considered how a piece might be framed on Twitter and Facebook – some gigs will have you writing social media copy for the article you've written. You can argue that your writing should speak for itself, and that's true enough, but just like we talked about building contacts on page 52, social media is so helpful in building connections – with other writers as well as editors. My feeds are filled with writers from all over the world. Talking, sharing, debating, sometimes having a bit of a spat, sharing recipes and books and ideas. I adore that side of Twitter, and Instagram, too. There's a community there and I love being a part of it. You get to choose where you spend your time as a freelance writer, and while for some of you social media won't stick, one of the most rewarding things you can do is find your people. I suspect a lot of them are hanging out on Twitter chatting about a brilliant article they read recently.

Using Twitter searches

Even if you don't use Twitter for anything else, you should be using its search function to find writing work. These are the most useful phrases to include in your regular search that will help you find calls for pitches and paying writing gigs. TweetDeck is a particularly useful thing for searches – just set the phrases up and they'll do the work for you. When you see a call for pitches that doesn't quite match the wording here, add it to your list. Use double quote marks around these phrases to search for each specific one.

- Call for pitches
- Call for submissions
- Looking for pitches
- Accepting pitches
- Send me pitches
- Send pitches to

- Email me pitches
- Email pitches to
- Call for writers
- Call for freelance writers
- Looking for freelance writers
- I'm commissioning
- Commissioning writers
- Commissioning pieces
- Commissioning features
- #journojobs

Freelance success story

*'I'm a bit of a finger-in-every-pie freelancer and even though I have publications I could keep writing for over and over and not need to pitch to new editors, I still find it thrilling to work with a new editor or see my name in a different publication. I feel successful when I manage to get non-traditional or 'out there' ideas commissioned and an editor takes a chance on something different. My happiest freelancing memories are those pinch-me moments when you realise, "Hey, I got paid to write about crisps" or "I was watching these YouTube videos anyway, now I'm paid to write about them!"' **Amelia Tait, freelance writer***

The last word

Every pitch you send makes you braver. Not because you're crossing your fingers hoping that it'll land, but because you're learning more about your voice and what you want to say. You might always have a little niggle in your confidence when you're pitching – every freelance writer does – but the more you do it, the easier it gets. It's a craft that you have to hone, just like any part of writing.

It's also an opportunity for you to shape how your freelance career looks. The more you pitch, the more time you spend examining what you want to do. You're not just a fashion writer or music journalist – you know exactly what it is that makes you tick. Pitching is the easiest way to make your freelance writing career your own, and that's where your daily joy lies.

Doing the Work

It's easy to forget about the actual work when you get a commission because you're busy celebrating your brilliance and dancing around the kitchen. Then before you know it, you're running out of time and your case studies haven't got back to you and the introduction isn't coming together and you're making a bit of a pig's ear of it all.

This chapter is about doing the work, but it's also going to make your life a little easier. It's not about stopping the celebration – it's never about that; goodness, carry on, you brilliant thing. Go for your nice lunch, take yourself out for a cocktail, pop to the bakery with the fancy cakes. Just remember that nothing takes the wind out of the sails of a nice lunch quicker than an email from an editor asking for a complete rewrite.

I didn't keep on top of the work when I first went freelance (well done to those readers who are noticing something of a theme to my early freelance years). A large part of this was because I didn't have enough work to fill my days, so I faffed about most afternoons. I enjoyed the free prosecco at events because it was free, and I was twenty-five. Being given free drinks on a Tuesday night felt a bit like Christmas. I couldn't believe my own good luck and I was enjoying the hell out of it. I also enjoyed sleeping in and starting work at 11 a.m. because

I had enjoyed too much of said prosecco. Then I wrote an article or two in the afternoon. Was I enjoying being a freelance writer? It's impossible to say – I wasn't actually doing any of the damn work. It will be blindingly obvious to you – although it wasn't to me at the time – that I was dealing with a lot of issues outside of my fledgling freelance writing career. I had no idea that my self-esteem was crashingly low. The truth was that I was too scared to pitch editors regularly. Too scared to do the actual work.

One day I gave up on the work completely. I showered, got dressed. I was just about to head out of the front door and then for no reason I got back into bed. Still dressed. With my shoes on. Two hours later I got a taxi straight to my doctor and was diagnosed with depression.

Several months later, when the anti-depressants started to kick in, so too did my work ethic. And now it's one that I am steadfast about: deadlines, word counts, sticking to briefs. I think we've established that I'm by no means a perfect freelancer, but I've learned that my work is a useful way for me to keep tabs on my mental health. If I'm having a tough time mentally, I can see it in my work. If my confidence has taken a knock, I'm far more likely to be playing the part of a writer and being all Carrie Bradshaw about things than meeting my looming deadlines.

I know I lost a lot in this time, and I try not to think about that too much. I let editors down, I stopped being fun to work with, I stopped being reliable, I missed out on work and I lost commissions. It bothers me sometimes, but all I can do now is move forwards and be incredibly thankful for all that I do have.

Building myself back up was a slow process. It meant putting the work in and trying something new. I discovered that not only was I good at the work, but I truly loved it. I wasn't just enjoying the idea of being a freelance writer, I was soaking up every little bit of it. I loved the challenge and the fact that I could create something entirely new. That's when I created my own platform. *Domestic Sluttery* was one of the very first lifestyle blogs in the UK. It launched in 2009 and blazed a trail long before influencers, before magazines had caught on to digital (it would be a surprisingly long time before that happened). I learned what doing the work really means when you're freelance. Not just about the late nights and the blood, sweat and tears. I learned that doing the work means that you get to be proud of the work. You get the joy of making something that only you could have created.

And oh, did I ever love being a writer once I stopped playing at it. The crafting, the ideas, the edits. I was showing up for all of it. Of course, my depression didn't magically vanish the minute I launched a website, but I felt like I was fighting back. My self-esteem took time to strengthen. I still partied harder than I should have, but I was beginning to find out who I was. Creating my own platform gave me something of value to focus on. I needed to show up and do the work. No one ever wants to hear that. Everyone's looking for a quick fix, a speedy way to the top. If you think a writer has been an overnight success, you haven't been paying enough attention.

I realised that the writing career I had been dreaming of wasn't about the idea of being a writer, it was all about the work that I loved doing. My definition of success – and my own happiness – was shifting. I realised that my career was very much in my hands. Yours is, too. If you're willing to put the work in.

What makes a good freelance writer?

There are dozens of writers in the world who are more talented than you.

That may not be a particularly inspiring statement, but it's the truth.

I'm not the best writer I know. I'm not even close. I try to be the best writer I can be. Freelancing isn't a competition to be the best writer in the world ever and you will exhaust yourself by lunchtime if you treat it like one. Being a 'good' freelance writer – one who gets regular commissions and repeat work – isn't always about being the most talented. It's about being reliable, turning in good copy, and doing what you're paid to do.

That means showing up at the page and doing the work properly.

Of course editors want brilliant copy, and stories that will inspire their readers and create debate, and – let's be honest about the business here – increase subscriptions and advertising revenue. If you think your job ends with a decent story, you're going to find it hard to make a regular living as a freelancer. If you aren't focused on the nuts and bolts of your job, it becomes very difficult for an editor to hire you.

That means working to a deadline. It means sticking to the agreed word count and being thorough with your fact-checking. It means not bitching when an editor comes back to you with edits.

Writing is about focusing on making your words brilliant, but the business of freelancing is about doing the job well. You need to be good at both.

It can be surprising to some freelancers but every editor I know has had to deal with a freelancer who has missed deadlines, rushed copy, half-arsed a feature and, in some cases, didn't bother to file at all. It happens surprisingly often. I'm still waiting for edits to a travel piece about Hampshire that I commissioned in 2015.

The job doesn't start and end with the main event. It's like a tennis champion turning up for the Wimbledon final without doing any practice. You can get dazzled by a few shots because they're naturally brilliant, but they can't stick it out for five sets. An editor will want to work with someone who puts the work in every single day.

Successful freelancing is often about doing what you said you'd do and sticking to the deadline you've been given. Take pride in your work. If you're not willing to do this, you'll get commissions but you're letting regular work pass you by. An editor can't commission a column from the writer who misses two out of three deadlines. If your copy comes in 1,200 words over the word count ('feel free to cut wherever!'), you've added two hours' work to their plate. Make it easy for editors to say yes. Not just to your pitch, but to working with you.

When my depression was at its peak in the early half of my career, the benchmark for my work shifted. I was just happy to be getting the words out; I stopped putting care and attention into them. You might get away with it for a couple of pieces – if you've been submitting good work, an editor probably won't mind reworking an intro or doing a spot of tidying up. As my mental health declined, the quality of my work was getting worse. The editor who gave me my first commission called me out on it and told me that they were finding it hard to take anything from me at all. I was still writing solid pitches and selling a story, but I wasn't delivering.

I bucked up. Quickly.

We all have moments when we can't juggle everything on our to-do lists, when the computer eats our work or we're unable to do what we promised. The only way you can get past those issues is if you've built a good relationship with your editors and to do that – you've guessed it – you need to be reliable every other time.

You don't have to be the best writer – you can learn from writers that are better than you; they're probably your friends. Reliability is about taking pride in your work. Even if you have two dozen deadlines due at the same time, your editors should never feel like they weren't a priority.

Writing a first draft is the easy part. It's the shaping of a piece that's the real work. And that's the work that a freelance writer commits to. If choosing the right words is about respecting your craft, choosing to be a professional writer is about respecting your industry and the people you work with. And it's your bread and butter.

How to keep going when you've got too much work on

Even if you've got amazing time-management skills, at some point you're going to end up with too much work on your plate. Whether it's saying yes to too many commissions or trying to juggle your freelance work alongside working full-time/planning a wedding/surprise home schooling in the middle of a pandemic, sometimes there is just overwhelmingly *too much to do*.

Maybe we're scared to say no to anything that comes our way. Every piece of work we get offered is an opportunity and some projects are impossible to turn down. Did I even think twice about saying yes to writing a piece for the *New York Times* when I had five other deadlines? Of course not. Unfortunately, work almost always takes longer than you think it will, especially if you're tired. (Ironically the task that I put off because I think it will take half the day usually takes me about ten minutes.) If you're in too deep, it's time to make a plan.

1. **List everything you have to do according to the deadline.** Plan this out on the calendar, your to-do list, your wall planner so you know where you stand.

   - Article about bees: 20th
   - Edits for ferret feature: 20th
   - Social media copy about butterflies: 21st
   - Ice cream feature: 24th

2. **List the stages of every project.** If you need information from other people, images or quotes, make sure these are at the top.

   - Interview for bees piece
   - Quotes for ice cream feature
   - Images for ferrets
   - Bees draft
   - Outline for ice cream
   - Butterflies copy
   - Butterflies images
   - Draft for ferrets

You can already see how this starts to change your plans.

3. **Plan these dates on your calendar.** When do you need to chase your potential bees interviewees to ensure you have the interviews done in time? When do you need to get those

ice cream images sorted? The goal here is for you to chip away at the tricky bits of your work, so when the time comes, it's just you and your blank screen and all you have to do is write with as little interruption as possible.

4. **Add in any other important deadlines or tasks you've got on.** Job interviews, your best friend's birthday, and for God's sake do your laundry. Anything that will take up time, even if it's not work-related, needs to be marked on your plan.

5. **Include time for a fresh edit.** You've got a lot on but make time for one final read-through with fresh eyes before you hit send. You can't be objective about your work when you're exhausted. Make a cup of tea.

Now you've outlined your tasks properly, you can see if you're going to struggle with deadlines and work out when you need help. If Tuesday looks so full your eyes might start to bleed, add a takeaway to your plan, or move that haircut appointment.

If you really can't juggle the amount of work on, talk to your editors. Be honest with them; don't make up some elaborate reason about why you can't meet your initial deadline, just ask if it's possible for a little more time. Most editors are understanding when you're upfront with them.

Writing under pressure is hard. Don't beat yourself up about taking on too much. Freelance writers are frequently underpaid for their work – when you're getting paid a few hundred for a piece and you're trying to enjoy your life, buy a house or pay for a holiday, it's hardly surprising that you're taking on too much. By finding a way that takes the pressure off for you, even a lot of work can be enjoyable.

Let's talk a little more about pressure

Even when I'm busy, it's rarely outside pressure that I struggle with. It's the pressure that I put on myself. No one was pushing me to start a new project, take on that feature for the *New York Times*, or write 10,000 words of fiction in a week alongside my freelance commitments. No one else is measuring my word count. We're all too caught up in our own lives to care about what someone else is up to.

When what you're striving for is difficult, it's natural that it starts to feel tricky. Making something of your own can be hard. The pressure that we put on ourselves can be useful – it can tell us what we really want. But our goals and dreams are meant to guide us, not drive us to exhaustion. Do you need to write 4,000 words of your novel right now? It's 3 a.m., you've only just filed your copy – what are you gaining from this? Are you doing that project because you want to, or because you feel like you have to? Who says so?

This isn't a get-out-of-jail-free card – that project won't happen if you keep putting it off – it's just a reminder to check in with yourself and where that feeling of pressure is coming from. Forcing yourself to sit at your desk when you're exhausted and hungry doesn't make for good work, and the work you do for yourself, however challenging, should delight and inspire you. That's a lot easier when you're approaching it with kindness and encouragement.

There's one thing I now know about pressure that I try to remember when I'm feeling up against it or being hard on myself: it's OK to just try. Not try your best, not try to be the best you can be all the time. Just to try.

Exercise

Do the thing on your to-do list that's bugging you.
You know the one. The niggly thing that you've been
putting off. It won't take anywhere near as long as you
think, and your mind will be much clearer when you've
completed it.

How to edit your own work

Self-editing is more than just a spellcheck (although if you're
sending your pieces to your editors without bothering to do
that, have a word with yourself). Your work needs a critical eye.
Meeting a word count shouldn't be our primary goal; that's a
numbers game. It's not our job to hit 800 words, it's our job to
make someone feel something, to inspire them, to create debate,
to convey a spark of something special. To tell a story.

You can't do that if you don't edit your work.

You need to make time for this. No matter how busy you
are, you need some time to step away from your work. So make
a brew. Or at the very least go for a wee – you've been meaning
to go for the last hour. Your first draft isn't anywhere near
good enough. If you don't read back through your work, you've
decided that your first thoughts, whatever words popped into
your head, are the right ones. If you believe this, I suspect there's
a little insecurity at play.

Here's a checklist of everything you need to do with your
first draft.

Read it again. And aloud

In an ideal world you'd print your work out before reading. A read-through on the screen you've been staring at for hours doesn't always cut it. Our brains fix our mistakes for us, so we don't see that missing word or that unusual phrasing because we know what we meant to type. By the seventh read-through you can probably parrot back your entire article, but it's only when you read aloud that you'll spot the typo in the third line.

Reread the brief

Have you done what your brief asked you to do? I've misread briefs so spectacularly that an edit has taken hours to fix. 'I spend a lot of time writing briefs and really thinking about what I want the piece to be before I commission it,' says *Cosmopolitan*'s Cyan Turan. While your brief is often based on the pitch you've sent, it's also been discussed and shaped in a pitch meeting to make sure it's just right. 'It's often also been approved by a more senior editor before it's sent to the writer.' Whatever you send to the editor needs to be what they asked for.

Have you written in house style?

The house style guide is a freelance writer's bible. Some publications go for the Oxford comma and others choose not to. A newspaper might have a specific way of writing a date, and they will all spell hummus differently. House style and publication tone are a real bugbear for editors. Make sure you're doing what you can to get it right in your draft. An editor shouldn't keep having to pull you up on their style guide. If a publication doesn't have one, refer to old issues, or make a note when an editor tells you their preferred way of writing. If in doubt, ask when you file so you can get it right next time.

Does anybody have any questions?

School essays and Carrie Bradshaw are probably to blame for our propensity to frame an article as a question. Make sure you actually answer the question that you couldn't help but wonder.

You're absolutely, truly, certainly, surely, very obviously bumping up your word count

Before I edited this book there were twenty-seven instances of the phrase 'here's the thing'. Cut all of the padding and the phrases that you overuse.

Write, then rewrite

Our ideas aren't always clear until we've started writing a piece. You can really strike upon something in the last 200 words. Don't leave your wishy-washy draft standing; rewrite the first half so it has as much purpose and definition as your final points.

Starting strong

You can do a lot with a killer opening line. Especially if...

Nailed it

... you've also got a cracking final sentence. Readers will stick with a piece because of the opening sentence but they'll share it because of a killer finishing line.

Tighten up

When you've cut all of your extraneous phrases, verbose sentences, adverbs and word crutches, *use* the rest of your word count. Editing isn't just about cutting down; you need to frame your words in the best way and say exactly what you mean.

This checklist is the practical one, but it's not the most important part of editing. For that you need to go deeper. Examine the structure of your piece – does it flow? Does it read well? Even in 800 words you still need a beginning, middle and end. Next, move on to how it feels. If you were the reader, what would you get from the piece? Have you done what you set out to do?

You have to straight up tell yourself when you're writing crap – you're padding because you haven't done the research, or you're writing woolly sentences around an idea you haven't developed enough. Learn to spot your own bullshit before an editor does. They can elevate your work, but this is so much easier when you've already done the heavy lifting. 'It's really important to be thoughtful in your work,' says *Pit* editor Helen Graves. 'A lot of work now is "bashed out" due to time restraints or the need to turn copy around quickly. The more time you can spend thinking about a pitch or a story, the better.'

The writers who are willing to do that work are the ones that will get repeat commissions. Choose to be the freelance writer who's willing to put in the effort instead of one who is half-arsing it.

How to handle a brief

A well-written brief is a freelance writer's dream. It outlines everything you need to do. It's a proper anchor that you can refer back to when you're getting a bit lost. When your brief is woolly (or worse, non-existent), you can feel like you're sinking.

You won't always get a proper brief. A rushed phone call might be all you get, ending with a breezy, 'Well, I'll let you get on with it!' and panic ensues as soon as you've hung up. What do you do if you're not given a brief? Write your own. Use your pitch, use the scrabbled-together notes from email conversations and phone calls. Then email it to your client to sign off, outlining the rate, word count and deadline again. Let them know that you'll go ahead and get started unless there are any issues with what you've outlined. If there's something not right, a client will tell you.

Tempted to stray from the brief? Don't be, or at least discuss it with your editor first. 'As a hired writer, you should be able to meet a brief, even if you'd personally like to take the piece you're writing in a different direction,' says veteran magazine editor Lara Watson. Even if you can see a dozen different ways a piece could go, the outline in the brief is always the right way.

What if the brief isn't right?

Sometimes a brief comes to you and it's entirely different to what you had anticipated. 'If you think the brief isn't right, raise it straight away,' says *Cosmopolitan*'s Cyan Turan. If you don't speak up, it's not your job to push the article in the direction that you wanted to. You can be creative and imaginative, but you have to deliver what was asked of you. You can't file a 4,000-word long read if you were asked for an 800-word listicle. Don't be like every writer character in American TV shows who take an entire week to write one feature and then file it while saying, 'This is a little different to what we discussed' (they are always commended for this; it drives me bonkers). An editor knows exactly what they need, what their readers are expecting and the space that needs filling. You're not 'fixing' or improving the article by ignoring the brief, you're setting yourself up for a rewrite.

How to deal with losing a client

The first time I lost a freelance client, it was... my only client. I got the can in a Starbucks – a perfectly bleak setting for such an occasion – then I hopped on a bus, met a friend and drank four massive glasses of wine.

I woke up with zero clients and an almighty hangover.

Now I tend to go for chips instead.

You are going to lose a client at some point, and it won't necessarily be because you did something wrong. Budgets get slashed, businesses go in different directions (and they go under), sometimes editors move on and the new editor just doesn't get on with your work in the same way. Reading this won't prepare you for it. Whatever the reason, losing a client feels personal. When you've committed to something, it's pretty crushing to find that someone doesn't feel the same way. If it sounds like I'm talking about ending a romantic relationship, it's because I think there are a lot of similarities. You've worked hard to nurture a connection, you've put the work in, you've got something good going. And then BAM! It's gone. Being dumped is no fun, whether it's personal or professional – you feel rejected, humiliated and like you could have done something to stop it.

Sometimes your clients will do it in person. It may happen over the phone. One of my clients ended our working relationship of three years via email (yes, it did feel a little bit Jack Berger and the Post-it note). Some working relationships just fizzle out.

If you can muster up the courage, asking for feedback can be useful – having an understanding about whether or not you screwed up, if there's someone else, or if it's not you, it's actually them. In the world of dating, we'd call this closure. See? It's not so different.

113

Make sure you wait a while before responding to your client. Just as you'd like your exit from a break-up to be calm and collected, graceful even, your email to your client should be the same. Focus on what's left to wrap up. Make sure you outline what's left on your plate – your last features, any edits that need doing, anything you need from your client before you can complete your work by the agreed date.

It's a good idea to invoice at this stage if you can. Outline everything outstanding and get it approved. Even the client who hounded you every hour for edits that weren't due until the end of the week can go a little quiet when they stop needing anything from you.

The last few weeks of a project is when some clients will try and squeeze everything possible from you – contacts, expertise, more copy. Don't forget: you only have to do what's been agreed.

Just as we change throughout our careers, so do our clients. It's highly unlikely that we'll write for the same publications throughout our lives, although we'll probably have some that we always return to. We often move to different publications as editors move about. If you freelance for variety and freedom, you don't necessarily want your week to look the same every Monday to Friday. A job ending isn't always a bad thing – we can even feel relieved. It opens up space in your schedule and it frees your mind up for something new.

What to do about the hole in your schedule (and your bank balance)

So now you've finished up, what's next?

You need to take stock of what money is coming in. If you've created a spreadsheet or finance tracker (more on that on

114

DOING THE WORK

page 174), you'll be able to see straight away how the shortfall will impact you. You can't fix anything if you don't know where things stand, and this is when your anxiety will creep in. We worry about the unknown.

Hunting for work can be overwhelming, but the following three-step process makes it easier. It allows you to take care of the most important and pressing issue first – the fact that you need some more freelance work – but it doesn't throw out your current to-do list. It's likely that while you're trying to replace your client, you've still got others that need your attention, so you're going to have to multitask.

1. **Complete tasks that are immediately practical.**
   Your first priority is to pay the bills.

   If you've got outstanding paid work on your to-do list, get it done before anything else. Feel great about still having work and being good at it! Send that invoice! Get money coming in. Chase any unpaid invoices while you're at it.

   Now it's time to focus on new work. Talk to the rest of your clients about taking on extra features – this is one of the easiest and quickest ways to get more work on your books. Get pitching. Rework your rejected pitches and send them out again. Apply for new gigs. Email that editor you've been meaning to contact. Follow up with the friendly editor who told you to pitch again. Let people know that you've got a gap in your schedule. Tweet about being open for new projects. Do what you can to make the work come to you.

   Almost every time I tell people I need more work, I get offered some. Don't pretend that everything is fine and you're super busy when you need a bit of help and have something to offer. Make sure people think of you when they've got something to commission. Be available to new opportunities. You can be all Ross 'I'm fine!' Geller about things if you like, but you're making it harder for yourself.

When you have done this, stop. Otherwise, you'll start panic-pitching and nothing can be gained from you searching the same jobs boards and refreshing your inbox over and over.

Now, just like your very own choose your own ending story (let's call it *Dave and the Unpaid Phone Bill*), you have a choice. You can down tools for the day or you can jump to stage two.

This is entirely your call. No medals are handed out for hammering out job applications for gigs you don't enjoy just so you can say you were at your desk for eight hours. Go for a walk instead if you'd rather do that. Or eat some chips.

2. **Complete tasks that will be helpful in the near future.**
Have you updated your CV recently? Have you edited your website? Do you have PDF versions of your features? (Try and get into the habit of saving these regularly; websites close with alarming frequency and when the hosting fees stop being paid, your work will vanish. If you think this won't happen to you, here's a cautionary tale: when I was halfway through writing this book, one of my favourite interview features disappeared from the internet forever.) If someone asked you to send them your portfolio, could you send them your best work in the next five minutes? That's what we're aiming for with this task.

Now's the time to give everything a spruce-up so when people do come looking for you because you're doing the work and putting all of those feelers out, you're looking as brilliant and dashing as you possibly can.

When you've done these things, you're done for the day. It's time for those chips.

3. **Complete the tasks that are aspirational.**

I know you're not thinking about your novel right now. You've just lost a gig. I get it. But there's a lot to be said for working on your dream projects when you've got some downtime in your schedule. 'Sian, I don't have downtime! I've got to find a job!' Yes, you have. But you've done the work. If you've done the first two tasks in this chapter, you're doing all that you can.

This third task is the one that stops you going mad with worry. It's a distraction, but a helpful one. Now's the time to get going on that newsletter you've been toying with, or the website/podcast/choose your own ending book club* you were thinking about launching. Otherwise, you're twiddling your thumbs and panicking about not having a job.

My newsletter *Freelance Writing Jobs* was born because I had a terrible six months where I didn't work enough. Massive chunks of my novel get written when I am between projects. Would it be better if a commission landed in your inbox so that you had something to write today? Damn straight. That's why you take care of steps one and two first. You're not burying your head in the sand.

This is the time to focus on the work you truly want to fill your days with. You need to keep pushing for the dream work to become the actual work. If you make time for it

---

* If you do launch a choose your own ending book club, I will be there with biscuits and a huge bundle of *Fighting Fantasy* books that I've been hoarding since 1991.

117

even when work is tough, it's always a priority; it's on your schedule all the time. If you always work on your book on a Friday afternoon, don't stop that just because you're looking for work. Treat your novel like it's your new client.

Working on something new and exciting keeps you feeling creative when you've had a bit of a knock to your confidence. Just as no one wants to shag you when you've recently been dumped because you haven't showered in five days and you've just found a chocolate button in your hair, no one wants to work with you when you're in a bit of a state and feeling sorry for yourself. So keep working on the things that make you happy. Keep your brain going. Remind yourself that you're actually great at what you do. Getting a commission or a job offer when you're working on something else feels good – you don't need the thumbs up from someone else to write, you were already doing it. This rarely happens when you're refreshing your inbox or staring at your phone and willing it to ring. When you busy yourself and focus on things that are important to you, good stuff happens. It's the professional equivalent to getting a text message from your crush when you're not looking at your phone.

When you have done all of these things, however long it takes, repeat the entire process. Follow up on leads and new things that have landed in your inbox since earlier in the week, chase new opportunities, pitch for new features. Then go back to your project. Then repeat it again if you need to. So much of the freelancing battle is to keep your focus and stop the anxiety from creeping in. Take it step by step; don't try to fix things in a day. You can't skip a step in this process or just hang out in step three for four weeks because you're having fun and thinking about real work is a bit scary. Every stage in this process is as important as the previous one.

Work will pick up again. Even in the hardest of times – pandemics, recessions, everyone pivoting to video because Facebook told them to. Freelancing isn't always easy, but we get through it and find a way. This isn't about being blindly positive – losing a client is a crappy thing to deal with. So if you need an afternoon to yourself, take it. Ignore people who tell you to 'look on the bright side!' if you're still sad and worried after a few days; your feelings are entirely valid. But also know that your next project will likely be bolder and brighter because you've been doing the groundwork. That page you added to your website will be the reason someone gets in touch. The tweet you were nervous about sending will catch someone's attention. You've been building your experience and your skills, and you've been making yourself look super appealing to new clients. You've put the effort in without even realising it, and those skills you learned in your last job haven't gone to waste, either.

Few things are inevitable in freelancing, but losing clients is one of them. The only thing you can control is what you do next. Eat the chips first, though.

How to stay focused

How many times do you stop in the middle of writing something? *Oh, I'll just see what's happening on Twitter. Oooh, an email.* Three or four? Maybe you'll write a paragraph and then go and open your inbox. *What's the cat chewing? Where did he get that?* While writing this single paragraph, I stopped twelve times. *Perhaps it's time for another cup of tea.*

I am very easily distracted. Lack of focus is an issue for a lot of freelance writers – we're used to spinning plates and juggling lots of deadlines – but it's a bit more than that. There's the idea that you're never quite doing enough. Rather than FOMO – Fear of Missing Out – maybe it's a Fear of Losing Out instead. If you aren't checking Twitter for calls for pitches, you'll miss your shot. If you're not reading every single email you get as it comes in, *whoosh*, there goes your big break! That dreamy editor will never discover your brilliance if you don't get that pitch done right now, even though you've got three pieces on the go and 11 billion browser tabs open. All valid, exhausting points.

I used to brush this off and tell people that I enjoyed working this way. I'm great at multitasking! I thrive under pressure! It's not true. Without realising it, I had succumbed to the cult of busyness. I revelled in it. I was in demand! My schedule was full! My inbox was fit to burst!

I was shattered.

While we'll all have times when there's a lot of work to juggle, working on fifteen things at once just isn't sustainable. We need to give our ideas the space to breathe. We need to give our work the time it deserves, rather than squishing it in at the last minute.

We know that the easiest way to do good and enjoyable work is to do it without added pressure, when we're relaxed. And yet! 'I've got all the time in the world!' suddenly turns into 'Where did all of my time go?!' and sobbing at midnight while still trying to write an article instead of getting some much-needed sleep.

Keeping your focus is hard, especially on work that's proving to be trickier than anticipated. My mind always wanders when I'm not sure of the next steps in a project. I'm also a big believer in the benefits of procrastination, but if you keep losing your focus, here are my top tips.

Make a plan when the work comes in

If you're reading this and your deadline is ten minutes from now, I'm sorry for stating the bloody obvious. It took me a long time to get this right. When I got a commission, I'd make a cup of tea/dance about/go out for lunch to celebrate, mentally (and often literally) spend my fee and then arse about for the rest of the afternoon. Now (as outlined on page 105) I make a short list of everything I need to do for that piece – interviews, image sourcing, ideas – and pop them on a calendar. I might not actually do the work straight away – I'm busy dancing – but I've at least started the work. My brain is in the right place, even if my feet are not.

Create an email rule

If you are fighting a losing battle against your inbox, make an email rule. Maybe that means only reading your email once or twice a day. Perhaps you only reply to urgent emails or put an auto-reply on when you're on deadline. Or you might simply delete work emails that arrive on weekends. I'm a sucker for inbox zero and given that so much of my business is actually email and newsletter-based, I try to make my peace with that. I do, however, regularly disable email on my phone. Your job isn't replying to emails; don't fall into the trap of letting it take over your life. For a game-changing look at how to respond to emails – or whether to respond at all – read Melissa Febos's brilliant *Catapult* article 'Do You Want to Be Known For Your Writing, or For Your Swift Email Responses?'[8] I reply to less than 50% of the emails I receive.

Work on paper

Don't even turn your computer on. There's nothing more

tempting than 'just checking' social media or email before you start work. If you don't need to be at your computer to get started on a piece, stick to paper and pen for a while. The flow of your words can feel great, even if you're surprised at how atrocious your handwriting is. The first half of this book was written by hand.

Break it down

Bitesize chunks are the best way to get anything done. When a task feels too big and overwhelming, break it down. This is such basic advice, but when I'm struggling, I forget the basics. You probably need a glass of water, too.

Focus on the things you can't control first

Don't leave your deadline in someone else's hands. There are some parts of the job that you'll need external help with, such as scheduling interviews, calling in products from PRs and companies for review, and requesting images. Tackle the bits of the job that you can't do independently before you do anything else. Your job is made much easier when you have everything you need in advance. Don't leave them to the last minute only to find yourself on the receiving end of an out-of-office message.

Plan your day, not just your week

I used to write a to-do list for the entire week, until I realised that I cherry-pick my tasks with abandon. I don't want to write that tricky pitch on a Monday morning! Let's do a fun project! Obviously, this leaves all the less fun work to Friday, and often the weekend. Now I break my weekly task list down by day, and I pepper the less fun tasks throughout the week. It works 80% of the time but for the times it doesn't...

... Bribes

If I get my piece of work done by noon, I can have that last chocolate biscuit. If I send that email I've been putting off, I can watch *Robin Hood: Prince of Thieves* in the afternoon. If I get my book edits done, I can order a kebab for dinner. The mind and heart are basic, and this method is incredibly effective. The kebab was great, by the way.

Work in short bursts

I'm always surprised by how much I can write in twenty minutes, and even more surprised to find that once I've got started, I'm usually happy to keep going.

Shut yourself out

When none of this is working, it's time to bring out the big guns. I use a browser extension called Self Control which locks me out of my email, my social media and any website that will distract me.

Know when to call it a day

Sometimes it's better to shut your laptop and call time early. Try these things first: eat a banana, have a glass of water, go for a walk. Then give it one last shot.

Dealing with edits

There are two kinds of writers: the ones who think they don't need editing, and the writers that editors want to work with.

Every writer needs editing

A good editor doesn't just catch a typo here and there or give your copy a polish. They can shape an article that's a bit flabby in the middle, they can make an overarching theme really shine. It's their job to make your words resonate with their audience and sit well within the rest of the publication, and if that means a complete overhaul then that's the right thing to do. An editor's job is to do the best for their publication and their readers, and in doing that, they make your work better.

This doesn't mean being edited is easy – every time I see my words changed and shifted about, I immediately think it's because I'm a terrible writer. They hate it! Why did they even commission me at all?! After I've had a cup of tea and a long talk with myself, I can look at a piece more objectively. Unless something has been drastically edited out of context, usually the edits are spot on. One of my favourite moments in my career was watching the late, great editor Pat Long hack my first piece for *The Times* to pieces as I watched over his shoulder, cringing. I learned a lot from that experience, and spent my lunch break comparing my draft and his edits to try and understand the changes he had made. It flowed better; it was tighter. That afternoon stays with me with every piece I edit. I don't leave the job to someone else.

Often you only see that you've been edited when you excitedly run to the shops to buy a copy of the magazine. It can be disheartening but those edits are usually a subbing choice – when images and headline text are added, along with pull quotes, it's a sub-editor who will edit your work to make it fit on the page.

When you get a document back with a note that says, 'Really enjoyed this piece! Just a couple of queries...' the colour rushes from your face. You'd ticked it off your list! You'd moved on to other articles! You were going to watch 'The One with the Holiday Armadillo' for the seventeenth time! No such luck – you're doing edits.

Here's how to make editing your work as painless as possible.

Don't complain to your editor

Complain to your partner. Your housemate. Your cat. Your WhatsApp group. Don't tweet. Do not moan to your editor. Your job isn't to file a draft, it's to submit a publishable article and until you've done the edits you haven't done that. You're still going to have to do the edits when you're done moaning about them.

Read the edits before you reply

Aaaah, people-pleasing. We can feel so bad about being asked for corrections that we just want to get them done as quickly as possible. Don't just fire off 'give me an hour!' to your editor without understanding what you're working with. You're not winning any points for being quick and inaccurate.

Clarify before you start

Pick up the phone if you have to. (I recommend this – hearing someone's voice is not only lovely and reassuring, but it helps get to the nuance of a piece that an email can't.) If an edit isn't clear, ask.

Be honest about when you can file

Editors know you weren't just twiddling your thumbs waiting for their email. Unless the magazine is going to press the next day, you probably have some time.

Speak up if you don't agree

You don't have to agree to a change just because your editor suggests it. Especially if it will dramatically impact the tone or meaning of the piece. There should be a little back and forth, and a discussion about whether you've tackled a topic in the right way, or if a point you were making comes across as you intended. If it's not clear to your editor, it's unlikely to be clear to readers. See the editing process as a collaboration. This is when you'll do your best work and it's when you'll have the most fun with your editors.

No editor is expecting you to be perfect the first time but they don't enjoy tidying up the basics; they want to get to the meat of the piece. You'll find that there are some editors who have a process you don't particularly like, but they're almost always right about what needs changing. Without exception, every writer I've worked with who complained loudly about being edited really needed editing. It's a lot harder to commission a writer who makes the editing process difficult.

You can make the process easier for yourself. Go back to the brief before you submit. Did you do everything that was asked of you? Did you do what you said you were going to do in your pitch? Have you filed the piece that was commissioned? Polish, be clear, and for goodness' sake run a spellcheck over things. Double check the style guide before you finish, too. Especially if it's for a new client. You won't remember every point straight away but after six articles if you're still being told the correct date format, you're making more work for your editor and they're right to be annoyed. You're going to have to make the edits anyway, you might as well do your best to get it right the first time.

Exercise

1. **Compare and contrast**. Print out a couple of pieces that you've submitted recently and compare them to the versions that were published. Look at what's changed. Is your intro tighter? Has the structure been altered? Are your 'jokes' cut? Are similar edits made to both pieces? Make a note of the pieces where similar edits happen.

2. **Look at the copy you're working on.** Are you still writing a woolly intro? Does your style of humour jar with the house style? (This is my polite way of asking if you're as funny as you think you are.) Don't ignore feedback when you keep hearing the same thing. Learn how to use edits to improve your writing.

Working with a tricky client

I would love to tell you that all your clients will be marvellous. For the most part, they'll be great. However, not every client you take on will be fun to work with. Not every client will be a good fit for you or your writing style. Some have the best of intentions, but their management style is tricky for freelancers. Here are some possible clients you'll find yourself working for:

The client who thinks you work for them full-time

You only work three days a month for this client, but they'll be in your inbox all the time with their bright new ideas that need your immediate attention.

How to solve this:

Often this client is just excited about your project, but their lack of boundaries can cause issues if you're not firm. You can choose to only reply during your agreed working hours, but it's often best to reply briefly and reiterate those hours. 'Thanks for sharing this, I'll look at it in more detail when we're next working together on Thursday.' If they still don't get the hint, discuss billing for your time. 'I'm happy to look at this in the next couple of days, just let me know and I'll add the fee for the extra time onto my agreed hours.'

The client who checks in every five minutes

You'd get your work done a whole lot quicker if they didn't keep pestering you about how your work is going.

How to solve this:

Your client is insecure about hiring a freelancer. Perhaps it's an intimidatingly big project or they're nervous because commissioning is a huge investment. They need reassurance that the project is going well, so it's your job to keep them in the loop. Reassure them that you'll update them on your progress at the end of each working day, and outline what your next steps are. Help them relax.

The client who makes terrible suggestions

You're doing a great job, but the client is asking you to make changes that are objectively awful.

How to solve this:

You can advise, but it's your job to give the client what they're asking for. I will push back once – very occasionally twice – if

I feel strongly about something. Explain why something isn't a great option for them and suggest an alternative or a compromise that takes their suggestions into account but steers things in a better direction. After a while, though, you just have to stop locking horns when the client insists on using an ampersand throughout their website text 'because it looks prettier' and send the invoice.

The client who keeps asking for changes

Your job should be done, but the tweaks and edits keep coming back all prefixed with the line 'Can you just...'

How to solve this:
Edits are part and parcel of any writing project, but you can put a cut-off date on the needless tweaks and edits if they keep happening. 'Let's get all edits done and dusted by Thursday so you're ready to go' should stop any repeated requests to move that comma back to where it was two days ago. If this becomes a serious problem and you're working with your client again, two rounds of edits should be enough so write that into your terms next time. Your client just wants to feel like they were involved. Or maybe they're a different kind of client in disguise:

The client who thinks they deserve freebies

The work you originally agreed to keeps getting longer with each edit, and 8,000 words has turned into 10,000 with no change to the agreed fee.

How to solve this:
Most of the time your client isn't trying to get something for nothing, they're just focused on the potential of the end product.

Be straight with them when they've reached a line that you're not happy to cross. 'I'm unavailable today, but I can make time for this work on Friday morning if you'd like me to book you in at the usual rate.' With clients that ask you for more than you agreed to, always bring it back to the rate.

The client who wants to pick your brains

You're not being paid to consult and it's not in your agreement, but the client invites you for a meeting 'to chat about things' and it's just to get your opinion on their business plan.

How to solve this:

Do you owe your client a favour? Are you happy for your brains to be picked for free? Sometimes you want to help your clients, especially if they've gone the extra mile for you in the past. Or do you just want to get on with the work you've been paid to do? Go back to what's been agreed. 'I'd love to take on more work with you, but let's focus my time on this project first' or ask for more money. 'I'm more than happy to discuss this at a time that suits you! My consulting rates are a little different to my writing rates...' You can test the waters with this one if you're not sure which way it's going – 'a quick catch-up' can almost always be done over the phone, which means you can be done in fifteen minutes. That's often more palatable than a two-hour round trip to give someone advice for free.

The client who drags their heels

While your client insists that your deadlines are immovable solid-stone structures, when it comes to something you need desperately – images, copy edits, extra information that you asked for three weeks ago – your client vanishes without trace.

How to solve this:

This is about boundaries and setting specific time aside for your clients. No client likes to think that they're not a priority, but being clear about the fact you have other responsibilities is important. When you ask for the extra information, give a deadline (earlier than you actually need it). When you follow up, explain that you cannot meet your deadline without this and suggest a new date. Usually, the suggestion of a later deadline – unacceptable to your client – will have them sending you everything you need. If it doesn't, meet the new deadline that you proposed. And invoice immediately – it's likely that this client will drag their heels on payments, too.

In an ideal world you'll have clients who love your work, love your edits, pay your invoice the same day you send it and then commission you again later in the week. Do whatever you can to keep these clients! With the rest, make your peace with behaviour that you don't love but can manage (and realise that you're doing things that annoy them, too). We aren't always in a position financially to chop and change our clients, but our freelance happiness often comes down to how you feel on a day-to-day basis, so managing relationships is something that can't be ignored.

How to spot client red flags

Not all clients are created equal. Some are a dream, but others might not have much experience working with freelancers and make the process much harder than it needs to be. Others will plain give you the runaround. Here are some clear red flags that while everything sounds good in theory, it's not going to be what you hoped.

They're woolly about the details

You have to tie down woolly details before starting the job, otherwise you're going to give yourself a headache. No end date, no firm budget, no clear idea of when you'll get the vital info you need – it's all going to be a hassle for you.

The person booking you isn't the person in charge of the budget

If you're not sure about the exact amount of money you're getting for your work, get it in writing before you start. The times when I have glossed over this step or confirmed budgets over the phone but not followed up over email have always been a mistake.

They won't give you a brief

A brief is so vital to ensuring that you're giving someone what they want. It also means you avoid thirty-six rounds of edits and dozens of emails with 'can we just change X'. Get that brief. I regret working with the client who didn't give me brief but instead told me: 'I don't know what I want but I'll know it when I see it.' That project was nothing but trouble from start to finish.

There's no agreement in writing

Don't ever start the work until you've got the brief, the rate and payment terms and the deadline in writing.

You've had three meetings and there still isn't any work

If you can, discuss the role over the phone before you have a meeting in person. If you've had three meetings and there's still no work on the table, you're basically acting as an unpaid consultant. If someone wants to hire you, they will.

The client isn't being straight with you

When you're getting to know a potential client, there are small telltale signs that something isn't right. You're told one thing but another turns out to be true, goalposts get moved, and sometimes, you can feel like you're being gaslit. Walk away; it's just not worth your time and your mental exhaustion.

You have that ick feeling

I can't tell you how many times I've ignored that feeling in my gut that a potential client isn't right for me. It's so obvious in hindsight, and I always kick myself for it afterwards. If it doesn't feel right, for whatever reason, walk away. I've never once regretted this. I have regretted taking on work that isn't right for me.

How to end a working relationship professionally

When a working relationship has simply run its course, here's how to end that relationship in a way that doesn't make you break into a cold sweat when you think about it three years later.

Choose the right method of communication

Although it's much harder, picking up the phone is often the right thing to do when you're ending things with a client. If you've only done one short-term project perhaps email is fine, but I've been let go from a couple of lengthy contracts via email and it's not fun. That said, if you think things are going to get difficult, email's the best option so you've got a record of everything.

Decide whether or not to tell the whole truth

It's not always easy – or helpful – to have a big discussion when you've decided to end something. Will it give you closure? Will it help you feel better about things? If you decide to go into detail, make sure you're prepared. Make some notes, stay calm, keep it about the work.

Be prepared for some clap back

Clients can take things personally when you decide to move on. If things get fraught, end the discussion quickly and politely. Remember, you've probably still got an outstanding invoice. Keeping things short and sweet means that you get paid with as little delay as possible so you can move on.

Wrap up in writing

Even if you talk over the phone, reiterate everything in writing. Including details of any outstanding work or money owing and dates when everything is due. Then wish everyone the best. Walk away with your head held high, even if it's the worst client you've ever had.

What to do when everything is going to shit

Some days you leap out of bed, have three commissions waiting for you, a nice email from a friend and a lovely parcel on your doorstep. Then there are days where your milk has turned and you didn't realise before you took a gulp of tea, the first three emails you read were rejections and two pieces have come back to you – one involving a serious rewrite. So what do you do when it's all going to shit?

When you've got something wrong

Fact-checking as a freelancer is vital. Some magazines will have sub-editors who will check and edit your work but for the most part it's down to you. There's little worse than having an editor pull you up on your facts. I have to double- and triple-check my dates in every piece – it's pretty embarrassing to have someone tell you that actually Henry VIII didn't die in 1957 (luckily this was spotted before going to print). No one's expecting you to be perfect, but you need to acknowledge your weak spots and look out for them. When you get something wrong, own up to it. Hold your hands up, apologise, and do everything you can to fix it quickly.

When your interview falls through

Always tackle the external elements of an article as soon as you can. This can't be stressed enough. I get a little bit nervous about approaching people for an interview, so often I'll put it off until much later than I need to, even though I love doing the actual interviews immensely. Don't make life harder for yourself, or your interviewee. And if it's at all possible, have a backup. Of course, if you're writing a profile you need to deliver on the interview you've been commissioned to write, but if it's a smaller part of a piece and you can find an alternative case study without too much hassle, this is a better option than going back to your editor and telling them that you can't do the story. The bottom line is that while sources and interviewees might let you down, it's your job to file your piece. Keep your editor in the loop and let them know that you've got it under control. Then deliver the best damn feature you can.

When your interview gives you nothing

I once interviewed a fashion model for a newspaper supplement and she gave me one-word answers, rolled her eyes at everything and was rude and difficult throughout the fifteen minutes I had with her. It was the worst interview I've ever done but here's the thing: the outcome of that piece was still on me. I let my discomfort get in the way of rephrasing my questions, repeating them, asking more firmly. I should have stood my ground – the interview had been agreed and I let her get the better of me. She still would have been a nightmare to deal with, but I'd have got a story I was happy with instead of having to file something I knew wasn't going to cut it.

When the PR isn't happy

At some point in your freelance writing career, you're going to piss off a PR person, or one of their clients is going to be angry about something you've written. Their aim is very different to yours. Your goal is to write a good story for your publication. Theirs is to get good press for their client. These things don't always align. It's a tricky balance – working with PR companies can help with so many stories, but your work is still independent. While you don't want to damage relationships, a good PR person will also know that you're just doing your job. The PR is also dealing with an angry client and just trying to fight fires. Don't let yourself be bullied by anyone – I was once told by a PR that the mayor of Tenerife was furious about a travel story I had written for a national newspaper and I was causing a nightmare across the entire island. There was nothing wrong with my piece, it just wasn't the angle they had been hoping for. I strongly suspect that the mayor had never heard of me, and I am probably still welcome to visit. Stand by your work. It's not wrong just because someone doesn't like it.

When you know what you're writing is a bag of shite

I'm sure you're a brilliant writer but sometimes a piece just doesn't come together, usually when you're incredibly tired or you've accepted a commission that isn't quite in your wheelhouse. In an ideal world you'll have some time to fix the bag of shite that you're staring at. Got a tight deadline? You need to step away from the computer, even if you don't think you have time. Reread your brief, give yourself some space so you can be constructive in your criticism (repeatedly calling it a bag of shite isn't always helpful). Does your piece do what you set out to achieve? Have you done what your editor asked? If you can answer yes to these questions, you're closer to fixing the issues than you think. Whenever I think my work is in a terrible state it's almost always a structural issue – I've usually written my way into the story instead of writing an outline. Reworking in a fresh document always helps. And picking up the beats throughout your story draft: where are the highs and lows? Does the reader have time to catch their breath? You hear this advice a lot, because it's brilliant and so often ignored: read your work aloud. I don't do this nearly as often as I should, but every time I do, I can immediately tell what's wrong with that clunky sentence.

If it's just not coming together, ask someone else to read it over and tell you what's wrong. They'll be able to pick up on things that you can't because you've been staring at the same piece for a week. Please remember that it's OK that this person is your editor. They're there to help you. If you can't get to the meat of a piece, it can be a really good idea to pick up the phone and discuss things instead of trying to second guess – you can lose a lot in translation over email.

The last word

There's no such thing as a perfect freelance writer.

Stop striving for perfection, it's not possible. What's more important than perfection is the willingness to improve. Being flexible and approachable and willing to learn and collaborate with other people – this is what makes a good writer; it's what makes you a freelance writer that people love working with.

Knowing your weak spots is not the same as drawing attention to your flaws. You don't have to be perfect, you do have to be willing to make changes to create the best work you can. Those changes can be introspective, but sometimes they're in the draft right in front of you.

Building a Career

There will come a moment in your freelance career when you'll realise it's stopped being about the hustle and the grind, and instead of ticking off a series of jobs, there's a genuine sense that you're building something.

You can *feel* this tipping point.

When you first start freelancing, there's an inclination to say yes to absolutely everything you're offered. 'It's an opportunity!' you think. 'I'm so lucky that someone even asked me to write for them!' and the classic: 'I have to say yes to all of the work – what if no one ever asks me to work again?!'

There is nothing wrong with saying yes to every piece of work you're offered. It's how you learn exactly what you want to write. That work shapes you more than you realise. Even if it's not a dream project, it's making you a better writer. Writing short-form copy for clients has made me better at editing my work. Marketing and copywriting for a furniture client paved the way for my love of newsletters and I learned early on in blogging that people are more likely to share your work when it's got a brilliant final line. You get to learn which bits of the job you enjoy most, and which you would rather avoid. Every feature you write helps you double down on what makes you feel fulfilled. When you start out, it can feel like you're just mindlessly ticking things off a list. The small steps are still progress! They're features, articles, bylines.

When you start honing your career, you're choosing what goes on your list. There's going to come a time when you have to cut some work to make way for something else that you love. This seems blindingly obvious, but when the work on your plate is perfectly fine and paying well, that's quite an intimidating prospect. When we make space for the work we really want to do, the more avenues and opportunities we're opening up.

When you tap into the bones of a long-term freelance writing career, what you'll probably find is a feeling of being settled. There's still a flutter of panic about where your next commission is coming from (honestly, it never completely goes away), but the feeling that you're on the right track is incredibly reassuring. When you know that the decisions you're making and everything you are doing are driving you forward, it feels right. This is how you build a career. It's not about how many articles you published in a year, or even how much money you made. It's a *feeling*, an inner confidence that you are making the right choices for you. You're back to finding your 'why'; you've been on that path all along.

Pinning down your goals and dreams

Freelancing shifted for me when I got smart about what I wanted out of my career. My goals only became clear when I took some time to pin them down. Spending time thinking about what you want isn't always easy – it means you first have to take a long hard look at where you are.

Some of my goals were obvious – I wanted to write more books (mission accomplished, go me!) – but I needed to put my finger on what I wanted to get out of freelancing, and where I wanted my career to go. So my goals stayed woolly for years.

Actually, they were so broad you could have driven a bus through them. 'Write a book!' 'Travel more!' 'Start a newsletter!' These aren't goals, they're dreams. Totally unhelpful in the grand scheme of things, but handy for small talk at parties.

It's time to narrow down your dreams and turn them into goals.

We don't have to seize our dreams immediately. It's nice to have some waiting for us backstage. At some point in my life, I think it would be lovely to own a little shop and I can picture it down to the colour of the tissue paper. I'm not doing anything about it. It's the dreams that keep us up at night that we should be paying attention to. This is why my lovely newsletter *Tigers Are Better Looking* exists. It's why this book exists.

Similarly, you don't have to shape your goals in one morning, and you certainly don't have to attempt them all at once (in fact, it's probably better if you don't try and do that), but getting comfortable with asking yourself what you want is a hugely valuable tool in your career. And the answers will surprise you. The world going into lockdown in 2020 made freelancing so much harder in so many ways, but it also helped us identify what we want from our lives and reconsider the things that don't matter so much. It's impossible to feel motivated about a goal that feels like it's from another time.

What's the difference between dreams and goals? The latter is actionable. You need to take control of them. And that means addressing every single step. I break my goals down month by month (thanks to some brilliant tips I've been following for years from *Real Talk Radio* podcast host Nicole Antoinette). Every January I write a list of career goals for the year ahead. At the start of every month I outline a small step that helps me get there. Nothing feels daunting or too big.

When you turn your dream into an actionable goal, 'write a book!' becomes 'finish my first draft'. This sounds the same, but the end goal is specific. Then each month, that's broken down further. 'Plot outline' in January, 'write the first three chapters' in February (it's cold, you've just paid your tax bill, you've got time). In March, you pull out the big guns and you complete your first 10,000 words. If you'd just leapt into trying to power through 10,000 words in January, you could have got there, but the little tasks make everything much easier. Your small steps help you feel successful, which is hugely motivating. You're on your way. In April you'll be closer. In July you might even be halfway there.

Your goals need to be determined by you. This is particularly hard for freelancers, when so much of the work we do needs the go-ahead from someone else, but when you're the one in control of your goals, you're the one in control of your own success and happiness.

Your goals can start right now. In a year's time you'll look back and you'll be amazed at how much you've accomplished. They'll be things that you truly wanted to achieve, too. As much as we'd like it to, life doesn't run year by year so you might not tick everything off your list – perhaps you're halfway through a book pitch, or your newsletter idea is still an idea scribbled in your notebook. You won't mind because either it's not the right time or, better yet, you'll be halfway there. What matters is that you've worked out what's important to you and you're going for it.

Exercise

1. **Write a list of everything – yes, everything – that you'd like to achieve as a freelance writer.** Nothing too big, nothing too small. Maybe you want to create your own magazine one day, or you've got a secret list of dream clients. Putting them to paper allows those big ideas to become a reality.

2. **Give yourself a rough time frame for each goal.** This helps you turn your dreams into tangible goals. Some of your ideas will be something attainable in a few weeks, others will be seriously long term. Don't forget that this is moveable! You are not failing if you need to shimmy stuff about. Life changes; our priorities are never set in stone.

3. **Break each goal down into manageable steps.** Our big goals can feel overwhelming, so it can be helpful to pull apart the goals into something a little more bitesize. I like to have a new task each month; you might prefer ten steps, or a weekly action to keep you focused.

Finding your niche

For every writer with a niche, there's another who seems to be doing perfectly well without one. I have always flirted in and around specific beats. I write travel features but I'm not a destination expert. I enjoy writing about design, but I'll never be called upon to cover London Fashion Week. I love writing about food and I regularly create delicious recipes, but 'food writer' isn't a label I'd readily give myself. I've tried to settle on a single topic several times in my career, but after a month of food writing, I'm itching to get on a plane or train. After a stint of travel features, I'll realise I've not tested a new recipe for weeks and I'll be hankering for my mixing bowl. I love the variety of freelancing and I want to do it all.

People get hung up on finding a niche when it can be more helpful to find what makes your voice unique. Whatever you're writing about, what makes your work special? This is why an editor will commission you time and time again – because they can only get your feature from you. It might be humour, your interview skills, or your unique angle when everyone's writing about the same thing. Think of it as finding your spin. When we find our spin, we're still writing pretty broadly – but we can really dig deep on a topic or angle. If you don't know it yet, the only way to find your own spin is to write more.

Sometimes you don't seek your niche out; rather, it's a logical step in your career. Lauren Bravo was already a well-known writer when her second book, *How to Break Up with Fast Fashion*, was released, but while she had always prided herself on not having a niche, she's now best known for her work in sustainable fashion.

'I'm easily bored by work, which is possibly what pushed me to go freelance in the first place. I always felt I could maximise my chances of getting work by being seen to have a broad range. A range that was still always pretty firmly in the lifestyle/ women's issues/pop culture realm, let's be honest – it's not like I was doing war correspondence one minute and a GIF-sticle about cheese toasties the next,' says Lauren. 'Though these days I suppose I do have more of a niche, I still feel grateful that I'm not wholly tethered to that topic. When I feel like I'm running out of ways to express the same point over and over again, it's a relief to be able to pitch a feature about sauerkraut or social media or sun cream instead.'

There's an undeniable comfort in finding your niche. Discovering that you can write authoritatively on a topic you enjoy covering is reassuring. It's also likely that you've got some pull in your industry area. You've got added value and that's what keeps the commissions coming in. 'I'm definitely very grateful to be at a point where commissioning editors will come to me and say, "We need a piece on X aspect of sustainable fashion, can you write it?" It's really nice to feel that element of security, that you're a small part of an ongoing cultural conversation.'

There is a flip side to having a niche. 'Not every niche is going to have the same marketability – if your niche is something you're also passionate about in your personal life, there's the risk you might wring it dry and ruin it for yourself a little,' says Lauren. When you focus on one thing – like covering a particular area of Italy, for example – you risk being pigeonholed. You might well love your niche and be more than happy to keep covering the same thing, but that risk is certainly worth bearing in mind. 'I am only one person with one brain and one voice, and it can get boring being asked to write variations on essentially the same piece over and over for different publications. Then there's the pressure to keep up with every new development, making sure I read every news report and stay abreast of every new stat.'

It's also worth considering how your niche might impact other areas of your pitching. 'I don't take commissions that would involve promoting unethical brands anymore, so naturally my pool of potential commissions is a *lot* smaller. Not every editor is going to want my "Hot trends for autumn... but all from a charity shop!" schtick. But thankfully some do. And I rarely turn down work that comes *to me*. When you're lucky enough to be on someone's go-to list, you don't want to jeopardise that.'

So now you've got into your niche, how do you get out of it again when you fancy a change? If you're a property writer interested in interiors or a food writer who wants to get into travel, the jump is simple enough. What if you're a beauty writer with an eye on business, or you're considering a move from the fashion pages to politics? 'Just keep on pitching ideas on other topics!' says Lauren. 'Getting into travel writing was really exciting for me, and I worked hard to build up good relationships with a couple of editors, taking a few big commissions back-to-back and pitching them often.

'When trying to carve out a new niche, give it as much energy and attention as you can, lay the groundwork, and then it will become a more reliable part of your arsenal in the future. Don't be scared to pitch on topics you've never written about before. It might be harder to win the commission, but ultimately if you can demonstrate your skills as a writer, and your pitches are good, plenty of editors will still be willing to give you a go.'

Try and find a stepping stone between industries to use your expertise in a way that serves you. Follow your beauty expertise towards beauty businesses or work your travel industry pitches so they cover food rather than beaches. Pivoting can feel drastic, but it's often more gradual and when you take very deliberate steps it feels much simpler.

There's often a tricky element of juggling, when you're a freelance writer, between the work you're doing and the work you want to be doing. It's incredibly hard to turn down paid work, and balance is something all freelancers will struggle with at some point in their careers. It takes time to establish new contacts with editors and publications and to build up a reputation alongside our existing work that's paying the bills. Freelance writers are impatient – it's easy for us to get ahead of ourselves but shifting your niche is when it's OK to have a plan and take your time. Those small steps you're taking are getting you to where you want to be.

Exercise

1. **Write down a list of your areas of expertise.** This could be one, it could be many things. If you don't have one, that's absolutely fine; look instead at the areas you enjoy writing about the most.

2. **Dig deeper.** Go further than just food or travel – what makes you unique? What are you doing that no one else is? Where are your strengths? What areas could you improve upon? What do you think is missing in the publications that cover what you write about?

3. **Work on five ideas in your niche.** Craft them using everything you learned in the last chapter and then send out those pitches.

Scoring repeat commissions

Anyone with an opinion can land a feature with a byline. This isn't enough to build a freelance writing career. You need editors and clients to come back to you time and time again. You need regular work and repeat commissions.

Freelancing seems chaotic to people who have full-time jobs. My family and friends think that I'm dashing about and writing here, there and everywhere. In reality, I rarely have more than five or six regular clients on my books and I'm more than happy with that. I may take on an extra gig or juggle things around, but the number of clients I have across a month remains pretty constant. When I've found a client I like – one that offers me fun and rewarding work, is easy to work with, pays on time – I'm happy to carry on working for that client for as long as possible.

When you have regular work, everything feels a little bit calmer. Pitching feels easier, work often comes to you. Two or three articles over a few weeks can turn into a regular gig, which means you can build a routine – on Mondays you have a set deadline, on Thursdays you block out your afternoon. You know how much you're getting paid for the month before you've even pitched anything. For all the talk about the freedom that freelancing affords, these blocks of regular work are gold dust.

Without building up regular work very quickly in my freelance career, I would have struggled more than I did. (Although to be honest, one of my reasons for regular work when I was starting out was that I was too nervous to pitch new editors and repeatedly pitched the same three people. Let's call it 'establishing relationships' rather than lack of confidence.)

So how do you get regular commissions?

The simplest way is by being upfront about wanting more work! So many of us are projecting an image that we're super busy all the time. We share our dazzling features on social media, we're all about overflowing to-do lists and exciting plans ('can't say anything just yet!'), and not once do we mention the fact that we're twiddling our thumbs a bit by Wednesday afternoon. Our desire to appear successful can work against us. Almost every time I've emailed an editor I love working with and said, 'Hey, that piece was fun to write, I would love to do more with you', it has resulted in more work – often with an immediate commission on reply. Sometimes you have to ask for what you want.

Before you dive straight into those emails, think about what it is exactly that you want and why. Do you just need more work, or are you after a regular column? Would you like a little more responsibility? Do you need more money? Knowing why you're asking a client or editor for more work helps you cement what you are offering them.

You also need to be realistic about your current client relationship. If you've missed deadlines recently, or your copy has been a bit scrappy, they're not going to be bending over backwards to give you more work. So consider how you hope to build that relationship and be honest about where you stand with your clients and what you're like to work with. Do you sulk or push back on edits? Do you watch deadlines whoosh by or go AWOL when an editor asks you to clarify something? Make sure you're delivering on your current agreement before you start asking for more.

Clients and editors want to commission the best work, but they're also looking for their days to be made easier and more fun. 'Be willing to collaborate!' says magazine editor Lara Watson. 'Be easy to work with, creative and take feedback well.' This is great advice whether you're looking for regular work or not, but collaboration is when great work can happen.

You can also try pitching a series rather than a one-off piece of work. This could be a batch of articles for a commercial client, or it could be three features on a theme for a website. Think about how the pieces work together, and what the client gains from this – don't just see it as a way to boost your monthly income. In almost all cases the batches of work I've done are for editors I've been talking to for a while. Building strong relationships is the answer to building regular work. It all comes back to 'reliability and ease to work with' says *The Simple Things* deputy editor Frances Ambler. 'You want to feel that the freelancer and the commissioner are on the same team.'

> ### Freelance success story
> *'Success for me as a freelancer looks like balance. The times when I feel most successful as a freelancer is when I have a regular contract gig, a few fun features or recipe commissions a month, all while I'm working on my long-term personal project. I need that regular contract gig because I can't relax or be creative without that stability, so it helps support the rest. I try and set goals and make lists of those dream clients or projects that I want to work with, and that really helps me stay on track.'* **Bre Graham, freelance food writer and editor of Dishes To Delight**

On originality

Most of the work that you create as a freelance writer will stem from your own ideas. It's one of the most rewarding parts of the job. Those weird little thoughts you have in the shower and on the bus that turn into brilliant articles.

However, when everyone is pitching on the same topics and hooking their pieces around the same news stories, you're probably having ideas in the same ballpark as other writers. What's crucial in being original is the execution.

Original execution is what keeps me creating. Making something new, trying something different. When *Domestic Sluttery* launched in 2009, no other blog was mixing interiors, food and fashion, something that's so hard to imagine now. When my newsletter *Freelance Writing Jobs* launched in 2018, it was the only jobs platform aimed at freelance writers in the UK.

You'll have no doubt heard the cliché that there are no original ideas. There are only so many ways to tell a love story. What's vital is how you approach a topic. This is what makes you interesting. It's what makes your work easy to commission. It's what you'll build your career on. When you see an article that's about a topic everyone's been covering, but it's come at the subject in a totally different way, that's originality. It's not about hot takes – we can all say something contrary for £150; successful freelancers do something *different*.

When you start out you will inevitably learn from other writers. A turn of phrase you like, a tone that you try to emulate, an opinion that almost sounds like it could be yours but isn't quite. You'll be inspired by articles, but not yet honed in on what makes your own work and your voice special. You might be lacking in originality, but this is part and parcel of learning your craft, and honestly, it's work that's best left in your drafts. You need to put effort into finding your own voice in your writing and working at discovering the thing that makes you... you. The only way to do this is to keep writing. Write and write and write until you've run out of paper and every pen you can find is dry. There really is no other way to get better at it. We write all the time in some way or another – emails, text messages, notes on the fridge to pick up milk – so to do it well isn't always seen as a skill. Just like any craft, you have to work at it to improve. It won't suddenly happen without you putting the work in. I spend hours working on my non-fiction, and then seem utterly baffled that my fiction projects are rusty as hell if I ignore them for a month. There's no easy route to success as a writer. You've just got to work at it.

'What if they steal my idea?'

There's a big worry that companies and editors will use your pitches without paying you for them. It happens a lot when you apply for jobs and the ad asks for you to send in 'three ideas that would be perfect for the magazine'. Your ideas are your currency; I recommend that you wait until you've had an initial interview before you start handing them out like cookies.

Although I've had my research lifted countless times by other writers and editors, when I started writing this book I was lucky that while I knew it happened in the industry, I had never had one of my pitches stolen. Then one rainy afternoon, while I was taking a break from a huge pile of paperwork, it was right in front of me. I was reading an article written by an editor that was *incredibly* similar to a pitch that I'd sent them a few months earlier. That sort of thing makes your blood run cold. The editor agreed that there was some overlap and apologised. There's no happy ending to this story. The respect I had for that editor was gone. I was left somewhere between furious and sad.

There are lazy, crappy people in every industry, but I don't believe that all editors are out to rip off freelancers and you'll have a tough time freelancing if you approach your career with this much suspicion. Pitch grabbing happens, but perhaps not as often as it seems. Magazines often commission months in advance; it's likely the piece was in the works for a very long time. When you're pitching around hot topics, finding hooks and ideas that are relevant right now, it's extremely likely that other writers are pitching similar pieces. When you read those pieces, they give you that awful sinking feeling in the pit of your stomach. *That's my idea. I pitched that.* Sometimes your suspicions are valid, but be aware that dozens of freelance writers pitch the same editors on the same beat, read the same press releases, look out for the same stats and studies – there is an inevitable crossover.

Look at it another way: when you have a brilliant idea but don't get around to pitching it, you'll see it on the pages of the magazine you would have pitched it to. No one stole this idea from you. You hadn't even told anyone about it. But there it is, making you kick yourself. You just struck on a good idea the same time someone else did. They just acted on it quicker.

So what can you do about all of this?

First up, **stop pitching editors who use your ideas without paying you**. If you feel uncomfortable working with an editor – for absolutely *any* reason – stop pitching them. If you have to psych yourself up to send a pitch because you just don't enjoy the conversation, or it makes you uneasy, just stop. There are always other editors to pitch, there are always other magazines that you will love working with and editors move around. It's just not worth the angst. The joy of seeing your name in a publication loses its shine if you don't enjoy the experience of crafting your piece. The bonus of being freelance is that you get to pick your colleagues.

It's so important to **pitch a story, not a topic**. We keep coming back to this, but it's so often ignored. When you're pitching a story rather than a vague topic, your piece has legs. There's a point of view, there's a fleshed-out story, there's something more to it.

A pitch with a beating heart is very hard to replicate, and as we discussed in the 'Getting Work' chapter, this is what makes your pitch a story that you are itching to write. When you connect to your stories, you write your pitches in a very different way. Make your pitches stories that only you can tell. Work on your voice so that when you pitch, it's entirely unique to you.

Lastly, **hold something back**. By all means discuss case studies, but you don't have to share contacts or immediately tell an editor who your sources are. You don't have to show your hand in the first email if you're not sure. You can still write a cracking pitch while saving something for a follow-up discussion.

You are always right to defend your work and your ideas, but think about all the things we've discussed in this chapter – how easy it is to have the same ideas, how similar the pitching topics are when everyone's going to the same sources. Where possible, it's always worth talking to editors a little more about your pitches when you do get a rejection. There could already be a similar story in the works, or you've just missed out because another freelancer just pitched the same thing. This has happened to me several times (and makes me feel guilty about my habit of procrastinating my pitching instead of just hitting send). This is a good thing! It means that you're pitching along the right lines.

Take something from the fact that when you've got talent, your ideas are something that you can always create more of (for more of that turn to page 48). You have them in abundance and you can rework your stories and keep coming up with something special. Not everyone has this ability, which is why they take other people's ideas in the first place. Second-hand stories will always read like second-rate stories. There's always a disconnect when someone is trying to pass off something that isn't wholly theirs. Rest assured that you're always one step ahead and the more you do to find your voice and make your work stand out, the better it will be and the harder it will be for someone with no imagination to replicate.

A brief note on plagiarism

If you lift from other writers in your career, you are not being a real writer. You just want that feeling of having written something, which isn't close to being the same thing. It is the epitome of laziness and smacks of contempt for the entire industry. The small sliver of success it brings won't be yours to own, it will belong to someone else. There are times when writers blur the line of 'inspiration' when starting out, but we all know what is right and what is wrong. If you know that you have plagiarised someone's work in any way, that awful sinking feeling should sit with you every time it pops into your head. You might change your ways, you may not get called out, and you may even get away with it, but you'll always know that you did it.

Establishing your brand

The phrase 'fortune favours the brave' is how I feel about self-promotion. Putting yourself out there can make you feel vulnerable, but when you do it in a way that feels good, you're committing to your work. You're standing by what you've written. You're showing up for your craft. Showing up certainly doesn't mean that you have to become an influencer. It doesn't even mean you have to spend half the day scrolling through Twitter or playing about with peonies on Instagram. Self-promotion isn't about shouting in the faces of everyone you meet, it's about finding your people.

The best part of social media – when it's not all drama, influencer scandals and disgraced celebrities publicly apologising for racism – is being a part of something. That community is much bigger than the piece you just wrote about that thing that happened to you that time.

Self-promotion can feel scary, but when you jump in anyway, you often get something back in return. By being brave and putting yourself out there, you're pinning a flag in what you do and telling people that you're good at it. You'll attract people who like the same things and editors who are interested in what you've got to say.

You learn so much from self-promotion. How to frame your work. You learn about who responds to what you're saying, and you learn how to say something in twenty words when you would have otherwise used 300. Most importantly, you learn to stand behind your words.

Not everyone is going to like what you do. I regularly get emails telling me what's wrong with my work, and I have things pretty easy compared with other writers. I've learned that if I'm proud of my work and it resonates with its intended audience, then I've done my job. Your writing doesn't have to be, shouldn't be, and isn't ever going to be for everyone. There's a relief that comes with accepting that.

Fear of self-promotion isn't about not liking Twitter or Instagram, or not having enough time for social media (although those feelings are perfectly valid). Often our fear is about being scared to get behind our work.

Consider this: self-promotion is the easiest way to showcase your writing. When you create your own professional website (which took me years, by the way), you're choosing exactly how you are being seen by potential clients. The work you put front and centre is your best. And after a while, that begins to become part of your professional brand. Your self-promotion isn't just what you share on social media – it's your email signature, the About page on your own website, the bio on the website you write for regularly. Creating a professional brand means creating a cohesive image so when someone comes looking for you, they know who you are and what you're about.

'But, Sian! I got my first six freelance writing jobs by people approaching me! I don't need to promote myself.' Well done you! It is entirely possible that you might build up enough of a reputation to have people coming straight to you, and if you've never had to pitch for work or apply for a gig, more power to you. But with a bit of self-promotion, you could be offered more commissions that pay more money. You could begin to carve out the exact writing career that you want, not the one that people are offering you. You get to choose. When it comes to freelancing, I believe that choice is where our success and happiness lies.

Some of you will roll your eyes at the thought of creating a brand, but you already have one (and right now it is someone who rolls their eyes at things they don't want to do). You're a travel writer, you're a food writer, you're a tech copywriter, you're a rock music writer who also writes a newsletter about their dog. You're a history writer who specialises in fashion but is also super into modernist architecture and would much rather be writing about concrete buildings than hemlines. You're a construction trade writer who is moving into writing arts and culture reviews. Maybe you're not sure of your own brand yet, but it's one of the best assets you can have as a freelance writer. And if you're particularly shy about self-promotion you'll enjoy it even more: it's all about putting your work first.

Exercise

1. **Write your website About page.** This task is never fun, but it helps you get used to selling yourself and highlighting your skills and talent. In 250 words, ask yourself what you want to tell people about your writing and your career. You're in control of this conversation – lead with that.

2. **In a short paragraph.** Narrow your About page down to a short bio. What's special about what you do? What's unique? What information highlights not just what kind of writer you are but *who* you are?

3. **In one sentence.** Sum up your professional brand – what do people know you for? What do you want to be known for? Keep narrowing this down until it can fit on a single line.

A side project by any other name

I absolutely love a side project. I despise the term 'side hustle'.

I hate the thought of hustling – the idea that you've gotta keep grinding; it's all work, work, work. A hustle is all money. Even the dictionary definition means to obtain something 'by forceful action' or 'to swindle'. That's not how I want to work. If I have to force my writing or hustle people to get them to believe in my work, something is off.

Perhaps this is little more than semantics but as writers, the words we choose matter. If we're going to spend a significant amount of time with a project, it's important to get that definition right. A side *project* – something you do in your own time that interests you – sounds like something I want to focus my energy on.

A side project when you're freelance is a glorious thing. It's the thing you dig out on a rainy Tuesday when you don't feel like working on that article, but you can't quite justify taking the afternoon off. It's the file on your desktop that you tinker with while you're waiting for feedback from a client. After you forget about it for months and then pick it back up you exclaim, 'Some of it's actually quite good!' to anyone within earshot.

The side project is, frequently, the dream work. It's the project that isn't always top of your to-do list, but you find yourself thinking about it more than the work that is. You whisper about it to trusted friends. Every time you work on your side project, you're working towards something for your future. There's no hustle here. There's a dedication to something we love when we have the capacity. Start that food newsletter you can't stop thinking about. Write your screenplay, launch your podcast, try out a short story, create your own magazine. No one works their best when they're hustling, but consistently showing up for your side project can be the magic that pushes your freelance career forward.

'I don't think of *Pit* as a side project anymore, and that has improved things immensely,' says Helen Graves, editor of live fire magazine *Pit*. 'When you work freelance, there's a lot of work to do that doesn't earn any money. There's research to be done, there are pitches to be written and there's a lot of time spent thinking of ideas or planning. The sooner you stop thinking about the financial side of this the better. It's so much more productive. *Pit* earns me money in other ways – it reinforces my niche and I get other work from it. It is a large part of what I do and something that I believe is very important, so I put a lot of time and effort into it alongside my normal work and consider it part of the whole. I also try to remember that I'm doing what I love, and most days I do remember that.'

Our side project is work that comes from the heart – the short stories, the newsletter, the poems you keep in a shoe box – that's our most intuitive voice. And we should listen to that voice because it's telling us what we need to work on to be happy.

Your side project also allows you to create something that doesn't yet exist. Food media has seen such a boost in new editorial projects over the last couple of years, largely prompted by the staleness – and whiteness – of the media's food coverage. With large food and drink publications under fire for shutting out particular ethnicities from content stemming from their own cultures (*Bon Appétit*, I'm giving you a hard stare right now), several independent publications that began as side projects are finding their audience. 'It's always been about platforming other people and unheard voices, different opinions,' says Anna Sulan Masing, editor of *SOURCED* and *Cheese, the magazine of culture*, who wanted to ensure that minorities and unheard voices in food have a place to tell their stories. 'I don't think that my voice is most important – my voice is only important when it's part of a context. I think that impetus is the drive to do these things.'

Figuring out what drives you – your why – is crucial to your side project not tailing off. It's what will help you keep going when Netflix is right there tempting you, or you'd rather head out to the pub. After a while – there's no set time, it's different for each project – that side project becomes something more tangible. It evolves into something that you can't ignore. It moves up your to-do list.

Freelance Writing Jobs was a side project that was born while I was finishing my modern literature MA. I had no idea it would become such a huge part of my freelance life. Even *Domestic Sluttery* was an accidental side project – it was going to be a test blog for a publishing company, but I decided to launch it independently. If you think a side project always stays the same, consider this: *Domestic Sluttery* ran as a part-time venture for years until I made the leap into running it full-time and wrote my first book of the same name in 2011. The website closed in 2014 and two years later I relaunched a newsletter edition with my co-editor Laura Brown. In 2020, we rebranded as *Tigers Are Better Looking* and now we have an award-winning publishing business. Phew! That's a huge evolution for one project, but that's my point: side projects change, they shift with your life and your career or sometimes they come to a natural stopping point. Your side projects can straddle your personal and professional lives; they need to serve you, not work against you.

Freelancing is unpredictable but having my own projects gives me a sense of purpose. I might not have any work on my schedule, but I've still got newsletters to send every week and that brings in regular money. I'm still working even if I'm not getting many commissions. I'm an independent publisher and, best of all, I'm creating something that's entirely mine.

A word about hobbies

I started ballet classes in 2018. My teacher Georgie tells me off for sticking my bum out when I plié. My pirouettes are wobbly. I'm *never* going to perform on stage. But God, do I love it. When I stand at the barre, I breathe, and I raise myself up and I forget everything else. I am just Sian. Not Sian whose travel feature is due the next day. Not Sian on Twitter, with photos of her cat. Not 'The Email Lady'. My mind isn't on the deadlines that are piling up, or that annoying email. If I think about work for even a second, I lose my focus and my balance. Ballet needs every ounce of my concentration. Despite my teenage performing arts phase and obsession with dance movies (*Center Stage* is my all-time favourite), I am not a natural dancer. I don't care.

What does all this have to do with writing? I needed a hobby. One that didn't involve staring at a screen. So much of my fun was related to my work – writing, reading, design, cooking. Ballet feels entirely removed from it. Now I protect my ballet classes more than anything else in my schedule. I carve out that time in my diary just as I would a regular client meeting. I am the client. I'm in need of a catch-up.

There's a notion that because we're freelance our time is money, but you do not have to sell every minute of your day, and not everything you love has to be monetised. When you don't give way to things that inspire you – books, museums, motocross, ballet, pastries – after a while you don't have anything left in the tank to give. Make time for your hobbies, you need them more than you realise.

Freelance success story

'I abhor nepotism, and have zero interest in fame, but there's a lot to be said for recognition, and also your reputation – look after it. People respecting and enjoying what you do, or being the go-to voice they know will do a subject justice. Readers telling you they can't wait to hear what you think, or they saw something that reminded them of something you wrote – sometimes years and years earlier. Success is knowing you can take a day off and not feel guilty, to allow the laptop to power down once in a while. (Maybe one day.) Success is the power to say no to

162

stuff that doesn't sit right, even if the money is good and you might never be asked again. It's looking at your body of work knowing every single piece has its place, that it could only have been you, that you no longer have to compromise. It's not always about money – although often it is, and rent still must be paid – but satisfaction. You did a good job, you'd do it again and, more importantly, there's a chance they'll ask for you specifically; every day brings new ambitions. It's not just about making a living, but being able to live with how you make it. Success means accepting that in that regard you may always be a work in progress.' **Justin Myers, freelance writer and author of The Magnificent Sons and The Last Romeo**

Diversifying your income

We're warned not to put our eggs in one basket. Yet when we're in full-time employment that's exactly what we're doing. When people talk about freelancing being unstable, how you could lose work at any minute, what they don't consider is that our income doesn't all come from one place. It's still daunting to lose a job and it can knock your confidence, but you've probably got some eggs doing just fine elsewhere.

I lost a regular job yesterday. A good one that covered my rent and bills each month. Rather than feeling panicked, I had a bit of a cry and then took stock of what was still coming in. When you know what's coming in and what's going out, you can focus on what you need to do (for more information about what to do when you lose a client, turn to page 113).

I was still bringing in good money because my income is

diversified. You probably don't rely on one area, one client, one company for your freelance income. You're a little more in control of where your money comes from. The media industry is as unreliable as it ever was – staff jobs get slashed all over the place – but to paraphrase one of the best episodes of *Seinfeld*, now you're driving the bus.

A single income stream works for many freelance writers, but it's not the reason I work for myself. The more I start to rely too heavily on one income stream, the more precarious it feels, like I'm holding on too tight. Almost every time I've done that, budgets have been cut or my contract has ended.

I know that some of you are thinking that you're a writer, you don't need to diversify. You know what you're doing and you like it. But that doesn't mean that you can't use your skills to mix it up. Some weeks I'm a freelance writer in the traditional sense. I pitch articles and I write them and send an invoice. There are weeks when I'm working on books, style guides or brochure copy for brands I love. Some days it's copy for travel companies, social media plans for cultural organisations, and creating newsletters for publishing houses. Then there are the afternoons when I'm teaching and hosting events. I do all of these things with my writing hat on – they're all connected – but they're diverse, too.

My freelance writing career doesn't look anything like it did when I started out and I'm so glad of it. Your ideas and dreams will change, your expertise will take you in directions you'd never anticipated. In diversifying your income, you're taking steps to protect your monthly revenue but you're doing more than just bringing in money. You're creating a well-rounded business. Publishing houses host their own podcasts, publish newsletters, print magazines and create entire websites – why shouldn't you take advantage of all of these, too?

You can make a business out of just doing one thing – and if you want to, just carry on – but you have more options available to you. Some of the best writers in the business also host podcasts and create newsletters and write brilliant books. Perhaps they shouldn't need to, although if we're going down that path, we should ask *why* writers aren't paid more for their work and *why* traditional media freelance rates have barely increased in a decade. We should keep asking that question loudly.

We are in control of our own careers, and we are in a position to see the potential in the opportunities that come our way. You don't have to say yes to everything – I've learned that social media copywriting is not my calling, and I don't listen to podcasts enough to start my own. You might find that those things make your heart sing, even though you still love writing features and copy. You can do both! We don't just pick and choose our work for financial reasons – diversifying can have an emotional motivation, too. Finding ways to fulfil elements of your creativity that you haven't tried before is a lovely thing. I would always rather try than wonder. Say yes to opportunity, stay curious. The ways in which you make your money might change from week to week, but you'll always stay interested in them. Keep looking for the work that makes your heart sing.

The last word

Even if you're the most diligent of planners, your freelance career will veer off from the direction you'd anticipated. Your dreams and priorities change, but often what seemed so important to you when you started out stops driving you. This isn't a bad thing, although strangely it can feel like we're losing something when this happens. What we're often doing is making way for opportunities.

Being open to something new is one of the most rewarding parts of being freelance. You might not have said yes to that lucrative copywriting gig two years ago, but now it's right up your street. Travel writing could become a stepping stone to food writing, or maybe celebrity profiles are where you find your calling. Perhaps a newsletter gig presents itself or you decide to launch your own publication. There's no right or wrong way to have your freelance writing career play out – if it's the right choice for you, it's the right choice.

Be brave. Say yes.

Money Talks

This book has talked a lot about the craft of writing, but it's time to get down to brass. Let's make some money.

For all the less tangible elements of being a freelance writer – the creativity, the inspiration, the ideas – there is a fact about freelance writing that I am 100% certain of: you cannot be a successful freelance writer unless you get to grips with your finances.

You can still be a good writer. In fact, you can be a brilliant writer. You'll even have some success, win some awards, get some fantastic commissions. None of this matters in the long term. If you bury your head in the sand about the financial side of your business, you are cutting off your potential at the source.

I wish I had learned this sooner.

This chapter will stop you feeling intimidated by your finances, and it'll help you start seeing them as an opportunity for becoming a success. Freelancing can feel very hand-to-mouth, especially when you start out. It's not all about how much money is coming in, more about being able to plan for when it's coming in and what's going out. If you don't do this, you'll piss your money up the wall as soon as every invoice gets paid. Or you'll be too scared to take your foot off the gas, never spending a penny when you do have it. I managed a combination of both when

I first went freelance – I spent my money like Elizabeth Taylor shopping for diamonds, and I never, ever stopped working.

Getting your finances in order isn't boring. It's admin, sure, but it's admin that helps you to grow. It's valuable. The month I took control of my finances and finally created a system that worked for me was also the month I realised I didn't need to work every single evening to make ends meet. My ends were already meeting, I just didn't know it. My planning also showed me that a low-paying client was taking up way too much of my time and I could be putting that towards something more lucrative – pitching for bigger features or working on a personal project. Financial knowledge is so powerful.

My freelance success didn't come from making more money. It came from getting serious about my finances.

Getting serious about money gives you a contingency plan. It's not just about getting £500 for that article about bees, it's knowing when that money will hit your bank account, so you don't find yourself on a beach in Greece with little more than a fiver to your name. There's little fun in realising you've technically made thousands of pounds in October, but it was for a flaky client and you won't see that money before Christmas. Forewarned is forearmed.

There are a lot of unknowns in freelancing. You can't always account for a client not paying on time or a long-term job ending unexpectedly. However, you can make sure you always know where you stand financially. This knowledge has an impact on every other aspect of your freelance writing business and your life.

You know when to say no to work you're unsure about.

You know when to say hell yes to a last-minute holiday because you can afford to take the time off work.

You know when to ask a client for more work or pitch more.

You know when to put down your notebook on a Monday afternoon and go and get a hot chocolate.

Financial knowledge as a freelance writer leads to security, control, freedom and success. You have all of this information at your fingertips – it's in your bank statements, your invoices, your client emails. So ask yourself, what is it that you need to know?

Should you ever write for free?

Working for free is such a hotly debated topic in the creative industries. I know that there are a lot of people who expect me to jump in here, toe the party line and yell 'NEVER WORK FOR FREE!!!' at every fledgling freelance writer I ever meet. Here's the rub: when I started out, I was writing for free.

I was twenty-three when I started writing for the website *Londonist*. I wrote for them for around two years before I got my first paid writing gig. I hadn't even thought about getting paid for my writing when I started. I was just enjoying writing about the city I loved.

I made lifelong contacts in the industry and lifelong friends. *Londonist* led me to my first paid writing commission – when a previous site editor was looking for freelancers, that's where he turned. It got me my first book project, as shopping editor for the *Frommer's London* guidebooks working with Mat Osman, editor of *Le Cool* (and yes, bass player for Suede). At *Londonist*'s tenth birthday party in 2014, a previous editor introduced me to a well-dressed man called Tom, who became my husband in 2019. (Just seven years after you write your first article, you could meet your husband! Actual model may vary.) One of the website's longest-serving writers was my best man at my wedding, and in 2021, I was his best woman.

I left *Londonist* when I got a paying gig writing about London. It was impossible to juggle the two and by this point I needed to focus on my freelancing. Years later, I rejoined the site for a regular freelance stint when they had overhauled their business model, got some investors and started paying writers. I know that my writing career could have happened if I was writing for a website that paid from the get-go, but I don't regret this time at all. I don't regret writing for free. I learned a huge amount about working in a remote team and the technical side of writing – using a content management system (CMS), hyperlinks, image rights. You often have to learn that stuff on the fly when you're freelance. I wrote hundreds of pieces. There are some I can't bear to look back on because I wrote them in my early twenties and they were objectively bad, but I learned how to develop my ideas and got to understand what made my voice unique, though it would be years before I started to feel like I'd found my own style. While the website had its issues – some of them certainly commercial – *Londonist* wasn't a huge company that was out to take advantage of fledgling writers. It was a community website that grew into something bigger than anyone who set it up had anticipated. I wish that my own website *Domestic Sluttery* had grown into something that paid its writers anything like a living wage, but it paid peanuts. I hope that I created a platform that was incredibly rewarding for the hugely talented writers involved but I'm very aware of the hypocrisy of me yelling, 'Don't work for free!' when I didn't pay my own writers enough money for them to pay their rent.

I believe wholeheartedly that every professional writer should be offered remuneration for their work, but not everyone who asks you to write for free, or for very little money, is out to swindle you. Sometimes people are creating something new and exciting, and that spark of an idea comes well before building a business.

Would I approach my career differently now? Hindsight is a wonderful thing, and perhaps I would have. The industry is very different, as it will be in another fifteen years. I hope that the next fifteen years will see freelance rates increase, but at some newspapers they haven't budged in a decade. There's a part of the freelance writing community that thinks that you're dragging the entire industry down if you write a word for free, and while I understand that viewpoint, I don't think things are always that cut and dried. Where's the nuance?

When publications are launched by women of colour – *Black Ballad*, *gal-dem*, *Aurelia*, *Burnt Roti* – they're carving out space that isn't there, giving women a platform because otherwise the platform doesn't exist. Low payments aren't perfect, but neither is losing outlets for crucial and under-heard voices. We work in an industry that is making all of the right noises about diversity but still isn't budging up to let everyone sit at the cool table. If the alternative is not creating at all, I understand why writers choose to create work for free. You don't wait for an opportunity to be handed to you when you have the chance to make your own. You do not have to hand in your freelance writer badge because you did an article for your friend's zine back in 2017. Damn right you get to be proud of that work.

There will come a point when writing for free stops serving you. When you need to be doing actual freelance writing and the unpaid project that you love is taking you away from that goal. The truth is that although there can be value in it, if you write and you don't get paid for it, then you aren't working as a professional writer in that instance. You can be professional in your approach, in your deadlines and the hours you put in, but you're a volunteer.

Volunteering can be worthwhile. But remembering this definition will almost certainly change how you approach working for free. If you're going to volunteer your writing, it should benefit you far more than it does the person or organisation you're writing for.

While I sat at my desk in the city, selling adverts in the back of an insurance magazine, I certainly didn't think anyone would pay me for writing. It can take a little while for you to get there, both mentally and emotionally. Do writers get commissioned without ever writing for free? Absolutely. Just like you can make it in the media industry without doing an unpaid internship – something I never did. Everyone's path is different.

The debate is skewed – the issue isn't with writers who want to get their work published; it's with the companies and systems that are set up to exploit creatives. When a large company asks you to write for free, or chooses only to pay certain writers, ask yourself not just what you are getting from this, but what *they* are getting. I once wrote a 1,500-word feature for a national magazine 'for exposure' and I do regret that. (Not having a budget is different to not budgeting.) We should be pushing for better industry standards and fighting the fight where it makes a difference. Call out companies who repeatedly ask writers to work for free: the newspapers and large websites that pick and choose which writers they pay, the luxe travel magazine that for some inexplicable reason doesn't pay writers for their first article. Lay the blame at their door, where it belongs.

Companies will tell you all the time about their 'great exposure!' – I get asked to do something for nothing at least once a week. The company has already found you because of your work and your reputation. They've already decided that there's value in working with you. You are clearly doing fine without them.

The biggest lie that creative people are told is that there's no money in what we do. That we should do it for the love of it. It is absolutely possible to make good money as a freelance writer and you do not have to suffer for your art. You do have to be smart about what you say yes to. Every piece of work that you write for free eats away at the time you could spend pitching editors and working on pieces that will pay your rent and your bills.

This is probably the only point in the book where I still haven't picked a side of the fence to sit on and I don't think I ever will. Unsurprisingly I am a huge fan of people starting their own newsletters and blogs and creating their own revenue streams. Own your content. Keep creating, keep writing. And whether it's your words or your wisdom that you choose to give away for free, make a deal that *you* are happy with. No one else can decide this for you.

Do you know how much money you're making?

One of my biggest problems in the early part of my freelancing career was that I didn't know how much money I was making until I did my tax return. I knew when I had some big deadlines coming up, I knew I was usually making enough to live on, and I knew when things were pretty dire. But could I tell you how much I was due to make month to month? No idea. That lack of knowledge was a huge reason that I fell on my ass.

Financial knowledge is a step towards financial security. It's what allows you to prepare yourself for your month or week ahead. When you know where your money is, you can make informed decisions. Do you really need to work on that pitch at midnight, or are you just doing it out of habit? If you know that you're doing alright for commissions, you could put it on the back burner and book a holiday. Or, you could pitch two more pieces that month because you want to stay in that fancy hotel.

Figuring out what's coming in – and what's going out – is like exhaling after holding your breath. It's how you find joy in what you do. Before you go any further, you've got to get to grips with your budget. Not tomorrow, or next week. Put this book down right now and start. You can't save money unless you know what's coming in and what's going out. So the first thing is to understand your outgoings – list everything, from that daily latte you buy when you go for a walk, to the amount you spend on snacks each week. There's no point saying your takeaway habit is twenty quid a week when you know it's double that.

You can use a banking app to figure out your outgoings, or you can make your own spreadsheet. Whatever you use, make sure you've covered everything. It's useful to make a note of what things can be classed as expenses, too.

When you've worked out what's going out, lay out what's coming in. Everything for the last year, and the month the money gets paid. Take a look at those months side by side – your incomings and your outgoings will tell you exactly where you're at financially.

Peaks and troughs

There are times as a freelancer when you'll miss having a monthly salary. There are many ways in which we control our freelance income, but when you're relying on five clients to pay you, pitching your work before you know how much you'll get paid and juggling projects that take longer than you'd budgeted for, there's a lot that's out of our hands. It's not always easy dealing with the peaks and troughs of being self-employed.

However you choose to record your income, it's important to keep track of what you're likely to bring in each month as well as the invoice total. If you get a dozen commissions on 29 June, you probably won't see that money until August, and if there's a long lead time on those pieces it's more likely it'll land in your account in September. Past me used to scream, 'But I made thousands in July!' as I blinked at my sad-looking bank balance.

Now I don't just track what I get paid, but when I'm likely to see those pennies. I make sure I factor in a client's reputation for being slack with payments, as well as payment terms (although it's incredibly rare I'll accept anything over thirty days, you might find that you're working with a lot of magazine clients who pay on publication). This means that I know when my peaks and troughs are throughout the year.

Summer can be a notoriously tricky time for freelance writers – editors go on holiday, magazines slim down and you might even take a break. If you've had a quiet August, you won't feel it until October. Christmas is often my busiest time of year but it's also a short working month, so I just about break even. That boost at the end of the year looks great on paper, but it never stretches as far into January as I'd like.

Your peaks and troughs will be personal to you. Ironically, writing a book about freelancing doesn't allow for a huge amount of freelance work; my bank account was nothing but dust after I'd submitted my manuscript. When I was juggling work with essays for my MA, I would get hit by an empty bank account two months later. You stop pitching, you stop writing, you stop invoicing. When you start pitching again, there's a huge gap between getting a commission and finally seeing your money. Make sure your financial planning factors this in.

Actually, sometimes tax is taxing

I want to be totally honest about the financial ups and downs of being a freelance writer. Which means I have to tell you about the time I almost went bankrupt. I'm not sharing this story to scare you, or with the intention of putting you off freelancing. It's in the hope that you'll make much better decisions than I did.

There's a big gap of time between when you go freelance and when you have to do your tax return. People will tell you to save for your taxes, but this gap plays a rather mean trick – you always think that you can earn more money in the time between whenever you're reading this and the payment deadline of 31 January. So it doesn't matter if you dip into any money you've saved. If you've bothered to save much money at all.

In my first year of freelancing, I didn't save anything.

I feel incredibly stupid writing that.

I am still astonished by how clueless I was when I made the leap into freelancing. I know that some of you more money-minded readers will think I'm an idiot. (I look forward to your emails!) You're right. Hindsight is a wonderful, brilliant thing. I was young and made some stupid decisions. I wasn't budgeting. I wasn't expecting my tax bill to be as high as it was and, of course, I hadn't factored in payment on account (more on that on page 184). I just didn't have enough money in the bank. So I called HMRC, confidently anticipating that they'd be impressed with my candour, and requested to pay in instalments.

If you've ever spoken to anyone over the phone at HMRC, you'll know that while they are helpful, a friendly and light-hearted chat is rarely forthcoming. Then came the sentence that still makes my blood run cold when I think about it.

'If you cannot pay this bill, you will have to declare bankruptcy.'

I don't remember much about what happened next, but I did end up paying in instalments. It made things much worse – some of you will have seen that coming. As we've already established, I was managing my finances terribly. My 'solution'? I turned to credit cards and short-term loans to ensure that I was making the repayments (you can't pay your tax bill with a personal credit card anymore, thankfully). There was a knock-on effect from all of this – the good people at HMRC had anticipated it: the instalments were cleaning me out each month, which meant that I wasn't able to save for my upcoming tax payment. I'd got myself into a horrible vicious circle that felt impossible to get out of. I still wasn't an established freelancer. I wasn't being paid brilliantly by any of my clients, I was being paid late, I was working myself into the ground each month. I was terrified.

It took me less than a year to become several thousands of pounds in debt.

The panic attacks started about six months after that phone call. I would regularly sit bolt upright at four in the morning not being able to breathe. I didn't know what to do, other than just work harder and harder to earn more money. In my mind that was clearly the answer to the problem. And when I didn't work, I drank a lot, because I was a nervous wreck about everything. Of course my drinking made the anxiety worse. I had no idea how to fix the mess I was in. My panic attacks worsened and became a fully fledged panic disorder which got so bad that I developed agoraphobia.

I can't remember much of that time now, to be honest.

So I can't quite pinpoint why it came to a head, why one day I'd decided that enough was enough, or how I found myself sitting in my bank manager's office, sobbing, as they told me that they couldn't help me – in trying to fix things myself, I had borrowed too much money too quickly. I was left with few options, and I was terrified.

I was also incredibly lucky that I had someone I could turn to, even if it meant opening up about the state of my finances for the first time.

My parents bailed me out. If that sounds simple, it certainly wasn't – my mum literally took out a loan to pay off my debt. My bad finance decisions didn't just impact me. It took me several years to pay the money back, and I still relied on credit cards for a portion of my tax return for years after. I'll always be grateful to my parents that they helped me when I needed it but that conversation was incredibly hard. I had moved out of home when I was eighteen, I'd lived abroad on my own twice. I was a successful writer making it in the big city! I felt like a failure.

I carried that with me for a long time.

While my finances were in better shape, I certainly wasn't. The damage to my mental health was long-lasting. It was years before I got my anxiety and agoraphobia under control, and my drinking. I also understand now just how rooted in my own financial security my mental health is. If my bank balance is unhealthy, so is my mind. It's so important to me now that I keep on top of everything and make good habits part of my work routine.

I cannot stress this enough: if you are freelance, you need to save regularly for your tax bill. It is part of your job. There is no other way of managing it. If you cannot do this with each invoice payment, or every month, then you need to face facts that you are not making enough money to live on, and something needs to change – either how you are living or what you are earning. It is always better to save more rather than less. Don't rely on that big contract that you're hoping will come in right at the end of the year to save you, because Sod's Law of freelancing means that it won't. Don't rely on chance with something as important as this.

I made a series of very stupid decisions in my twenties but don't scoff at this story and think that it can't happen to you. Getting your finances in a tangle can happen within a couple of months. Perhaps two or three clients don't pay you on time, then a big job falls through – that's enough for you to eat through a chunk of your savings. If it happens again – as so many writers saw during the pandemic – the gap between payments can be big enough to cause some real damage. That's when you stop saving for your tax bill, so you're short a couple of grand at the end of the year. It can happen much quicker than you think.

Having trouble with your finances doesn't make you a bad person or a bad freelancer. It doesn't make you bad at your job; it's just one element of it. But it's a very, very important part. Earning more money isn't the answer; how you approach your money is. The only way you can get a grip on your taxes is to face them head on. Some of you will take to this so easily you'll wonder what all the fuss is about. Some of you will have to fight all your natural instincts not to bury your head in the sand.

I'm no longer a head-burier. I've gone from being someone who would cover their bank balance on the screen of a cash machine to someone who knows to £10 either way how much money is in their bank account. I now have savings, a mortgage and a pension. It's taken years to change my habits and I've needed a lot of support. You can't always manage on your own, but the changes I've made have been my own and I'm proud of them.

I wish I'd known that the person who would benefit most from all of this was me. When you understand your finances and know what you're earning, what you're paying in tax and where your money is, you can make decisions that work for you and help you live the life you want to. If we're defining our freelance success as financial freedom, it starts here.

Tax questions

Your tax return is one of the biggest things you'll have to deal with as a freelancer. It can be completely overwhelming but once you've done it, it's a huge weight off your mind. Although the online payment deadline is 31 January in the UK, you will sleep much better if you've done the paperwork sooner – you can file on 6 April, the day after the tax year ends. It's much easier to save towards a figure rather than blindly hoping what you've saved is enough.

Every return is different so we're not going into every stage of the paperwork but here are some useful pointers.

Expenses
There's a lot of grey around what you can claim on your tax return as a viable business expense. Don't feel guilty about your

expenses – you have overheads just like any other business. Your expenses aren't free money – you've still paid for your goods, you just don't pay tax on this. So if your turnover is £35,000 and your expenses amount to £5,000, you'll only pay tax on £30,000.

Here are some areas that you may not have considered (just make sure you keep the receipts for everything).

Magazines
All of those magazines you buy for research before you pitch a publication are a business expense.

Equipment
Need a new Dictaphone for interviews? That's a business expense. Computer needs replacing? That too. You can't do your work without equipment. And that goes for all office stationery, too. Even that cute notebook you bought with the rainbow on it.

Rent and mortgage payments
You can't whack your entire mortgage on your tax return but if you work from home, you can work out what portion of your home is deemed by HMRC as office space (the self-assessment website tells you exactly how to do this).

Utilities
The same goes for your electricity and heating bills, too.

Training
Signed up for a webinar? Gone to a training session? That's

all good. However, your training must be *wholly necessary* for your job, so that shorthand course gets the thumbs up but that expensive MA you've got your eye on probably isn't deductible, sadly.

Travel

Good news, jetsetters. As long as you're travelling to do your actual job, not just hopping on a bus to see a pal, you can expense your fares or your petrol. You can also expense hire car fees. This includes site and client visits, but travel to and from your place of work isn't an expense, so if you've got an office or desk elsewhere, you can't claim for that.

Hotel stays

Although you can't expense your holiday to the Algarve, you can expense overnight business travel.

Subscriptions

If you're a member of the IPSE (Association of Independent Professionals and the Self-Employed) or NUJ (the National Union of Journalists has a freelance arm), you can expense your fees. And if you've signed up to any professional newsletters or services, they're all deductible.

Marketing

If you've paid for adverts on social media or in a newsletter, these are also an expense. So are your professional website fees or any costs involved with sending your newsletter.

And some things you definitely can't claim…

Client entertaining

You could definitely do your business without taking your clients for a fancy steak dinner. Let them pay instead.

Your entire mobile phone bill

Your phone is mainly for work, right? Look, if you call scrolling through Instagram at 1 a.m. work then who am I to quibble? If you don't have a separate work phone, you'll need to work out a percentage of your mobile bill. That weekly call to your gran isn't on the ticket.

Expenses can be confusing. Especially when so much of our business is us and our lives – that indie food magazine you bought might have been for work but you read it in the bath and it was fun. Your home office is definitely your place of work, but what about that hour every morning when you cosy up with the cat and read emails in bed? If you're a food writer, those ingredients for your recipe testing are deductible (but that doughnut you bought with your eggs isn't). Our professional and personal lives are undeniably merged, and this is something that makes a 'one size fits all' approach difficult.

In cases when you're not sure, the HMRC website is pretty clear on what is and isn't a business expense. For anything else, it's helpful to put yourself in the mind of a large company when you're approaching your expenses. The CEO of Pret doesn't stump up for stamps out of his own pocket. Consider this example with each element of your business. You can run on a shoestring, but you don't have to – your business shouldn't be costing you money, but it should have outgoings. Realise that it's OK to invest in yourself and what you do.

What is payment on account?

You're going to get a surprise with your first tax bill. **There's going to be an extra 50% added to it.** I know, I know. There's a good reason for payment on account, but it has the capacity to trip up even the most diligent of freelancers. Payment on account ensures that you aren't paying your entire tax bill in arrears. HMRC uses your tax calculation to estimate what your bill will be next year. When you pay your tax bill in January, 50% of next year's payment is added on top. Please, please don't forget to factor it into your savings.

There's a second payment on account, too

Just when you think you've nailed your tax payment, there's another payment on account to remember that you need to pay by 31 July.

Can I change the payment on account?

If you know for certain that you're not going to make as much money from freelancing on your next self-assessment – if you're working in-house three days a week and have been paying tax through an employer or PAYE, for example – then you can change the payments on account. However, you can't just do this to pay less – if when you do your return you haven't paid enough, the outstanding amount will go on your bill, and you'll be charged interest for the amount you've underpaid.

Working on PAYE

If you work shifts for a newspaper or magazine, it's very likely that you'll be put on PAYE. If you're in it for the long haul, having someone deal with your tax for a portion of your income is certainly one less thing to worry about (and you'll accrue paid holiday, which is always lovely). If you're only doing a stint for a couple of weeks, try and push for invoicing – the paperwork and payment system admin just isn't worth the hassle.

Keep all of your payslips (the final one is particularly key), and when your tax return comes around, make sure you declare this income. You won't pay tax on it, but it does increase your turnover, which ensures you pay the correct amount of tax overall.

What else will I have to pay for?

Student loan repayments
When you're salaried, if you earn over the threshold (which changes slightly every April), any student loan repayments are deducted straight away. When you're freelance that's not the case so it's added to your tax bill.

National Insurance
There are two different classes of National Insurance for the self-employed. As an example, in 2020 you would have paid Class 2 if your profits were £6,475 or more a year and Class 4 if your annual profits were over £9,500. The amount you paid would depend on the class – £3.05 a week in Class 2, and for Class 4 it would have been 9% on profits between £9,501 and £50,000. For anything you earned over £50,000, you would have paid 2%.

This sounds like a lot of money coming out of your earnings, and it is. These are all things that we don't usually see as employees. They're all listed on payslips but all we really care about is our take-home pay. It's tricky for a lot of freelancers to get used to the idea that not all of the money that lands in their account is theirs. The money you invoice for isn't all yours to play with. If you choose to ignore this, you're likely to get stung.

None of this is meant to scare you. I say it to prepare you. Make sure you're on top of vital things: submitting that tax return early, saving for it and paying your bill. This might not be how you want to spend your weekend, but you earned that money using nothing but your grit and talent, and when you see it in black and white, it'll make you feel pretty damn proud and successful as a freelancer.

Should I be a sole trader or limited company?

At some point you'll have to make the decision over whether or not to become a limited company or remain a sole trader. Often the decision depends on the work you are doing. If you do a lot of work with corporate clients, or have longer contracts, a company status can look more professional.

You also remove any personal liability when you have a limited company. Your business is removed from you. And this means that any company debts are not your personal debts. You can also pay yourself a salary, and you won't pay corporation tax on your wages – they're a deductible business expense. If you choose to pay yourself dividends rather than a salary, you don't pay any income tax on the first £2,000.

There is significantly more paperwork with a limited company, particularly if you decide to become registered for VAT. You'll need to register with Companies House and do two different tax returns – your self-assessment and your company accounts. However, if you're on top of your paperwork, running your freelance business as a company can have positive impacts.

> ### Exercise
>
> **Make a tax savings plan.** Will you set up a new account with an automatic standing order, or siphon off money from each invoice? Work out what you're most likely to stick to. Then stick to it. There's no time too soon to start saving for your tax bill.

The tricky parts of a freelance income

There's a reason that freelancers pay less tax on their income: we don't get the same benefits as full-time employees. Here are the benefits that you need to factor in when you're working for yourself.

Holiday pay

If you're working regularly for a national media company, you might well be put on PAYE and accrue some paid leave, but in most cases, holiday pay is unlikely. That means you need to factor it into your turnover. When you're setting your day rate, make sure you work out a percentage for your holidays, too. You can do this easily by working out how much holiday you'd like to have per year – traditionally we'd take five weeks, but there's nothing traditional about freelancing so if you want to take two months off every summer, do the maths and make sure you can afford to!

We can kid ourselves that we don't need a break – it's especially easy when we enjoy our work. But not allowing for holiday pay means that you never stop working. It took me five years to take a real holiday when I first went freelance, and honestly, it was pretty sad. When you know your peaks and troughs, you know when money is good and when you can afford to take your foot off the pedal. And you'll know when you can afford to take a day for your mental health just because you need to. Duvet days are often written into full-time contracts because employers are starting to understand just how valuable they can be. Sometimes you need to take a day – at the end of a big project, or when you've been writing particularly difficult features, or you've just parted ways with a tricky client, or just because you've had a few too many late nights. Our holidays aren't just for two weeks on a beach, they're there for our own self-care. When you're freelance it's your job not only to make sure you can afford to take them but to make sure that you do. Don't be a crappy boss.

Sick pay

Getting sick is a huge worry for freelancers and it's more likely to happen if we don't take holidays. We often think that we can't afford to take time off, which in turn means we're not resting enough and that leads to exhaustion and not taking care of ourselves. It's not surprising that we can suffer from colds and sniffles if we don't give ourselves time to recover when we are sick or to take regular breaks and keep taking care of our bodies.

Maternity pay

Maternity rights in the UK are objectively terrible across the board. For freelancers, they're particularly bad. And for men, freelance paternity pay is non-existent. Our government believes that men who freelance have *no right to paid leave* if they become a parent.

If you take time off to have a baby when you're self-employed, you're entitled to statutory maternity pay. For example, to be entitled to the full amount in 2020 – either £151.97 per week or 90% of your earnings (whichever is lowest) – for the full thirty-nine weeks, you need to have been self-employed for twenty-six weeks out of sixty-six. If you haven't made any Class 2 National Insurance payments, you'll be given a grand total of £27 per week.

The good news is that you can pay any outstanding National Insurance in a lump sum, so you're all topped up and good to go. The bad news is that this can take weeks. First you need to wait until you're twenty-six weeks pregnant, but if there's an issue with your lengthy claims form, your full maternity allowance may not be in place by the time your leave is due to begin. The Department for Work and Pensions isn't known for its speedy response time. It's not unheard of for maternity pay to kick in long after babies have arrived. It's not a brilliant system.

There's also a certain amount of unfairness for freelancers around work they can do on their maternity leave. If a full-time journalist goes on maternity leave and decides to pick up an extra freelance commission or two if their contract allows, that is absolutely fine according to the rules. Self-employed writers aren't allowed to do this. Of course, new parents might not be particularly keen to take on commissions just after a baby has been born, but the differences between the two systems are galling. Instead, freelancers get 'keeping in touch days', which sound great in theory. But you only get ten of them. And the time isn't cumulative so even if you've only been on the phone for five minutes, that's one of your days used up.

It is incredibly hard for women to keep a freelance business going and have a baby, and frankly, the odds are hugely stacked against self-employed women returning to work. Communities like Doing It For The Kids and campaigns such as Pregnant Then

189

Screwed do amazing things for working women's rights, but it's not a surprise that many women decide to make the most of company maternity packages before going freelance. You might also decide to still work one day a week, or to take a shorter break than you might have if you were in full-time employment. Maybe one day we'll have a government that fights for women's rights and understands self-employment. Until then, when you start planning your family, make sure you get your paperwork in order as soon as possible and try to save some money alongside your maternity pay if you can. That buffer will help you relax so you can enjoy your leave with your new family. The well-being of you and your newborn is the most important thing to focus on.

Pension contributions

When you work for a company full-time, they pay into a pension scheme with you. A fixed percentage leaves your salary each month and it's matched by your employer. It's usually a good deal – far more generous than the government's offering. As a freelancer it's unlikely you'll be offered a pension scheme by your employers (although if you're PAYE and working a lot of newspaper shifts, you might well get the option). So you need to take care of this yourself.

It's hard to fathom your bus pass years when you're in your twenties but the sooner you start paying into your own pension the better. If you haven't done this yet, please don't feel guilty about when you start. There's no such thing as being 'too late' to start saving money. Take some solace in the fact that you're not alone – according to a survey by the National Employment Savings Trust, only 24% of all self-employed professionals are actively paying into a pension scheme.[9] I was well into my thirties before I set up my own! Yes, starting early is better, but whatever amount you're putting into your pension every month is better than nothing at all. Not starting because you already feel behind is a bit like not leaving the house when you're already late to meet a friend for dinner.

Freelance pensions are often flexible so you can change the amount you're paying in and pause payments if you're having a rough couple of months. There are so many options available to freelancers now and this wasn't always the case, so you can shop around and choose which is right for you. Whichever you choose, if you're a sole trader the government will give you a 25% tax-free top-up on your contributions. If you're paying in £100 a month, you're getting an extra £25 on top. Even over ten years, that adds up. Setting up a pension, even a small one, will be the smartest thing you do today.

How to get more money for your work

'There's no money in freelance writing!' is a phrase that you will hear a lot. People who are not writers will tell you this. Other writers will tell you this. Surprisingly, fellow freelance writers will also tell you this.

It's not true.

There is *plenty* of money to be made as a freelance writer. Sometimes it will come to you, but often your job is seeking it out. While there's money to be made, there is also a balance to be struck – not every part of the writing industry pays brilliantly. If making large sums of money as a freelance writer is your goal, there just isn't enough time in the day for you to do it by writing articles that pay £120 a pop. It doesn't matter how quickly you can write, this is a surefire way to exhaustion.

So here's how to switch things up so you get the dream work that pays:

Pitch publications that pay what you want to be earning

You will have clients that pay above industry rates. You will also have clients who might not pay well but give you work that you love. When things are swinging your way, you'll land a client that pays well for work that you love doing. The maths is simple. If you want to prioritise earning more money, you've got to make room for the work that pays.

If you want to be earning 50p per word, or £1 a word, you need to stop pitching and writing for publications that only pay 20p per word. To get paid more than £30k a year, you have to reduce the number of shifts you do that pay a low day rate.

There's nothing wrong with this work – or these publications – but this is about going for what you want, and when money needs to take priority, that can mean letting some things go. I know that I could make more money by writing more business copy, but it's not the only thing I enjoy writing. On the other hand, I love the work that I do for smaller arts and creativity publications, and while they tend to pay less, I'm not giving it up any time soon because I get so much creative satisfaction from that side of my work. You have to figure out what's right for you. Sometimes it'll be the money, other times it'll be the art. It's OK if you change your mind regularly; this is a very case-by-case sort of deal.

Only work for clients that pay you on time

It's easier said than done but working for clients that pay you on time is crucial to boosting your income because it changes your relationship with money. Working with late-paying clients makes it very hard for you to accumulate savings and build a pot of surplus funds. Chasing clients all the time also stops you feeling successful. When I've got money leftover at the end of the month, I feel like I can actually do something with it. I can build a future.

I get to live my life.

It's hard to do that when you work with clients who drag their heels on payment. No matter how much I enjoy the work, that's not always enough. Refusing to work with late payers is difficult – the commission is right there in your inbox – but remember that the money only exists when it's reached your account. If it's going to take five months of chasing to get what you're owed, it might not be worth it.

Put your rates up

When was the last time you increased your rates? The recommended NUJ day rate for doing freelance digital work is £175 although most news shifts are around £150. I don't think that's enough. Your expertise is what you're selling when you set your day rate. If you decide that your day rate is £150, you are capping your annual income at around £35,000 before deductions. Don't wait for the occasional client to offer more; do it yourself.

Ask for more money

Sometimes you have to ask for more money. If you know that what you're offering is worth more than you're being offered in return, make your client aware of this. Don't just say yes to the first rate you're offered because you're excited about the work. Question it. If it's a regular client, look back at what they've paid previously. If you've written a similar piece of work for twice as much, tell the client. If your deadline has a very quick turnaround, make sure that's factored in. You won't get more money every time you ask, but you'll never get more if you don't speak up.

Ask for more than your bottom line

Clients will always try and haggle you down, and if you've started at a low rate, you might have to go even lower to bag the client.

Exercise

1. **Conduct a client audit.** Look at each client in turn and consider the work, the time it takes and your rate. Do these things align? Does each client reward you financially or satisfy your ambitions?

2. **Increase the work with the clients you're happy with.** Can you pitch more or can you meet with your editor to discuss increasing your work?

3. **Reconsider clients that aren't working for you.** Ask what could change. Can you charge more? Can you rethink your workload with them? Some publication rates are set in stone, but it's always worth talking before you let go of a client.

You don't have to do anything drastic or rash if a client relationship isn't quite working for you – I'm not telling you to fire all your clients at once! – but you can make a plan to begin moving in a different direction. Look for publications in a similar field that pay more, start sending pitches elsewhere. Give yourself a time limit – say, three or six months – to replace your client with one that serves your needs better.

If you do this regularly, your rota will hopefully be full of clients you love working for that pay what you deserve. It's about more than just getting money to survive; you need to be able to live your life as well.

How to negotiate

We can tie ourselves in knots trying to put a value on our work and deciding what to charge. We don't mean to undersell ourselves, but we're often scared that we'll be told we're charging too much. That we're not worth the fee we've quoted.

There will always be people who aren't willing to pay what you charge; that is the nature of business. When someone says 'that's too much' what they're actually saying is 'I can't afford it' and those are two very different things. I can't afford couture but what Dior charges for a dress is very much their business. You don't want to work with clients who keep trying to shave pennies off your rate here and there because they aren't seeing the value in your work.

How to ask for more money

There's a phrase around freelancing that I've always bristled at: 'Always ask for more.' On the face of it, this sounds like a great idea. Ask for more! You're sticking it to the man! Get yours!

Always asking for more without thinking about it can sometimes mean that you're taking the piss. Like when your friend offers you some of their chips and instead of taking two you take twelve.

So what's the alternative?

Always ask for what's fair.

If you think the editor or client has underestimated the amount of time the research will take, explain this and ask for more.

If there's an element of exclusivity that adds more value to your work, highlight this and ask for more.

If you know that other writers have been paid a higher rate for similar work, talk to the editor about this and ask for more.

If you think you deserve more, ask for more.

Whenever you're asking for more money, back it up. Blindly asking for more means you're often just holding out your hands and hoping you'll get something for nothing. That's not a strong way to negotiate. You need to give an editor a reason to place more value in your work. You should see negotiating as part and parcel of freelancing but building strong relationships isn't about demanding whatever you can.

Why freelancers should talk about rates

We don't like talking about money, but transparency benefits every freelancer. When freelance writers talk to each other about rates, the industry opens up. You'll find out that, actually, you should have got fifty quid more for that article and you'll kick yourself if you find out after the fact. It might mean that you got paid to be on a panel when someone else didn't (this happens a lot!). The freelance writers who didn't get their money are all too often women and marginalised groups who are systematically paid less than their white male peers. Gender equality in freelancing has improved, but the gender pay gap still exists. The

Office for National Statistics reports that this currently stands at 17% for full-time employees. However, the gender pay gap for self-employed workers is much higher: men are earning an average of 43% more than self-employed women.[10]

We can only improve this when companies are transparent about rates, and we encourage this when we are open about what we are paid for our work. Sharing our rates holds companies to account and in doing so, we lift up all freelancers and help everyone put more value on their words and their time.

Talking about money isn't easy, but you don't have to be aggressive about transparency. You could say something like 'I had a chat with another freelancer who was paid £50 more for her recent opinion piece around the same length. I'd love for us to agree to the same fee before I get started.' There's no accusation, it's just facts. And they're hard to argue with.

There are some reasons why a writer has a higher rate – longevity with a company or editor is one, super-quick turnaround is another. Or the writer is white. A study by the National Council for the Training of Journalists (NCTJ) showed that 95% of freelance journalists are white.[11] While budgets are tight and editors aren't out to swindle their writers, writers of colour still lose out. However, for most freelance outlets, we're led to believe that the word rate is the same for everyone when that's very rarely the case. Get talking and share with your fellow freelancers.

Should you ever lower your rates?

Lowering your rates can be so tempting. It's an easy way to lock the client in.

Stop to think before you say yes.

You're agreeing to a rate that is lower than your worth. Once you've agreed on a rate it's very hard to increase it in future.

I once got asked to lower my rate for a project by a big travel client. I'd done a few large jobs for them, but the projects were research heavy and had a very quick turnaround. I enjoyed the work and there was talk of a more regular part-time role with the client when they asked me to come down on my usual rate. This gig was dangled like bait, and I took it. I knocked £50 a day off my usual fee – and when the project was complete, I was ghosted. I was £400 out of pocket by the end of the project. I don't think I even got a thank you.

I wish I hadn't been so keen to please. I wish I'd valued myself and my work more. I've learned not to negotiate about money, but about what I'm offering. If a client can't afford a 4,000-word project, take the project down to 3,500 words instead. If image research was part of the job, bargain with this. In breaking down what you do, your client will see what you are doing for the money. You're not saying no, you're giving them options based on what they can afford.

It goes a bit like this:

Client: 'Can you come down on your rate a little?'
Freelancer: 'Sure, we can look at a lower rate. For £3,500 I can do ten days, rather than twelve.'

Or this...

Client: 'My budget is really tight, can you do it for £2,000?'
Freelancer: 'I totally understand your budget constraints, so let's agree to 4,000 words instead of 5,000.'

Rather than bargaining with your money, you're reducing your output. The value in your work hasn't reduced. And that's key for a freelance writer. If you reduced every client quote by 10%, you could find yourself hundreds of pounds down across a week. If you're reducing your commitment, you're gaining time without losing money. Time for a new commission, a long lunch, video games, afternoon sex.

If you do decide to discount, mention this as a line item on your invoice. Don't just list the rate, show the reduction. Make it clear that your rate hasn't changed. Don't gloss over the fact that you know what your work is worth.

The trouble with invoicing

'Hiya, just wanted to check on my invoice for the piece I filed in June – it doesn't appear to have been paid? Only, it's a little overdue now.'

I don't complain about freelancing much. It would be odd to write a book about being a freelance writer if I didn't completely love what I do, but there is a bugbear that freelance writers all over the world share: getting our money. Without a doubt the hardest part of being freelance is getting paid. At times this has been bad enough to send me back into full-time employment.

I would love to tell you that it's just a handful of shady clients who won't pay you on time (or at all), but I've found that it's actually the largest companies who are notoriously bad at paying their freelancers, despite an editor's best efforts to ensure your money arrives quickly. When you do chase, you often hear the dreaded words 'we'll add it to the next payment run', which means that you're left waiting yet another month for your money and there's little wiggle room. Smaller companies are usually in a position to fix an error quickly.

The knock-on effect that this has on freelance writers – on freelancers in all industries – is huge. It's an especially difficult adjustment when you're used to a monthly salary. You could be waiting three, six or even twelve months for an invoice to be paid. I know freelance writers who have been fighting even longer. You can find yourself still freelancing for a client while you're waiting to get paid. It's exhausting, and it can send you into debt. Missed rent payments, missed bills, special birthday dinners that you have to skip because you can't afford the restaurant. It all takes its toll, emotionally and mentally as well as financially.

Trying to nail down why payment issues are so common across so many different companies is hard. It can be because of a company not valuing its freelancers. Sometimes it's forgetfulness. It can be because an editor is slammed with work and didn't process the invoice. Often, it's because of the good old payment systems. I talked earlier in the book about how great systems are, and there is an exception to this rule: it's every single payment system that has ever been created.

Every company you work for will have a different system. They are rarely effective. If they were, late payments would be few and far between rather than a widespread problem across all industries. These systems all differ in various tiny ways. Companies can ask for ridiculous amounts of information before you'll get paid, 'to get you on the system', but in many cases you won't be told about the one crucial piece of missing information required until your invoice is already a month late. In many cases, people are making it up as they go along. Then the whole process starts from the beginning, for reasons no one can explain.

Take heart in the fact that it's not always like this. There are some companies that pay as soon as you invoice! I don't think all clients who don't pay their freelancers on time are run by terrible people, but in so many cases payments to freelancers are seen as optional until someone gets around to it. You can tell a lot by how a company deals with overdue invoices.

So, is there anything you can do about not getting paid on time? Legally, yes!

Your legal rights state that you can charge a late fee of £40 for invoices where the total is less than £1,000. The fees increase to £70 for anything over that, up to £10,000, when you can add a charge of £100. You can also charge interest at 8% plus the Bank of England base rate to every invoice as soon as it is thirty days overdue.

That should be the end of the matter, but it's not that simple. I've *never* received a late payment fee. Usually, the threat of a fee on top of the invoice is enough to get a company to finally pay (and send you a snippy email). While a lot of freelancers have been luckier in getting their fees, in almost all cases you're burning a bridge so it's a last resort. Some companies will refuse to work with you if you charge a late fee – even though you are legally within your rights to do so.

This is where things get messy. Our editors aren't the people paying the bills but they're often our first port of call when our payments don't go through. Not only are we talking to someone who can't directly fix the problem, but getting upset and angry doesn't help our working relationships. It's incredibly difficult to strike that balance between 'please commission this pitch!' and 'FOR GOD'S SAKE, DEBBIE, YOUR COMPANY OWES ME THREE GRAND, I'M LIVING ON DRY CEREAL AND CAT LITTER.' The dynamic becomes so skewed when an editor is entirely reasonably asking for edits, tweaks, rewrites and you're sitting on your sofa crying about whether your invoice will be paid before your rent is due.

It comes back to value. Freelance writers are forced to jump through hoops to get what they're owed. We did the work, the client accepted it, we deserve to be paid on time. That's the barest level of a contractual agreement and I still cannot comprehend why there aren't industry regulations in place to ensure that this happens. The emotional labour involved in chasing payments is overwhelming. One global publishing company only pays invoices after a freelancer has chased twice. That's their policy. That's what freelancers can be up against. Some companies hope that you will give up – when you're invoicing for an article that you got paid eighty quid for, it doesn't always feel like that fight is worth the emotional strain. I can't make that decision for you, and while I know that every freelancer is entitled to the money they're owed, it's not a surprise that some freelancers make the decision to move on.

If you're reading this and thinking that I am exaggerating to build a narrative, ask the nearest freelancer. We've all got stories and we're all sick to the back teeth of it. Late payments are the worst thing about freelancing. Occasionally I get told that I 'knew what I signed up for' when I decided to freelance, but what this means is that some people think it's right for a company to withhold money for work that they're profiting from. I just can't agree.

Although it's not usually the fault of a freelancer that payment is late, there are some things you can do to help your payments go through:

Ask your editor for a contact in the finance department

To avoid bugging your editor about payments, ask for a contact, and not just 'finance@largecompany.com'. This is especially helpful if your editor is on holiday and there's an issue with your payment.

Ask your editor how great the client is at paying

Editors know when they're working for a company that takes months to pay its freelancers and most of the time they'll be upfront about it. I've been that editor and it's embarrassing. I would rather someone was upfront with me about when a payment will arrive. If you know a company drags its heels you can plan for it. In some cases, it might also stop you accepting the work at all. If I take these commissions, I view that money as a bonus that will be used for holiday money or a cute dress, not money I need to pay an urgent bill.

Ask when you accept the commission if you need to be added to a payment system

Give as much information as you're asked for. Then fill out the form that they forgot to send you a week later when they've 'moved to a new system' which will feel remarkably similar to the old one and your invoices will still keep getting lost.

Ask for every bit of information you need to add to an invoice

This doesn't always stop the invoice suddenly needing another piece of information – a very obvious stalling tactic – but it'll help.

Ask for confirmation

Not only to confirm that they've got your invoice, but also that it has everything they need to pay you.

Ask about how payments work over Christmas and bank holidays

Some clients will ensure you get paid before Christmas; others will shelve all freelance invoices to January without a second thought. I've had Christmas ruined by false promises so make sure you know what you're dealing with.

I absolutely hate that for freelancers this is a huge cross to bear but forewarned is forearmed – when you know you're accepting a commission from a client that takes three months to pay, you can plan for it rather than it being a financial shock.

You will still work with companies that pay freelancers late – too many of them do, it's almost impossible to avoid – and you'll juggle late payments with the rest of your admin. It can suck the joy out of your day. Yet I still say yes to the work. I will still work with a client I know pays badly but only when I'm doing alright financially. When I'm short on cash I'll work with a client that doesn't pay a brilliant rate but pays the day I invoice. You weigh things up and make the right choices for you, but factor in your time, too. If you've invoiced £350 for a feature but you know you'll probably spend another six hours chasing the accounts department, it's not a great rate.

No one is perfect and mistakes happen to everyone. Editors can forget to file your invoices. Sometimes you're working for a company based in the US and they forgot to tell you about the national holiday, so no one got paid that Thursday. How companies deal with their late payments is incredibly telling. If a client makes you feel bad for asking for your money, if you're given false promises of 'by the end of the day/tomorrow/next week', then you're going to find yourself utterly exhausted by it all. Worse than that, you'll feel like your work is being devalued and that you're in the wrong for asking for what you're owed. Don't fall for it. Get your money and run away from that client as fast as you can. And then warn other freelancers.

While getting paid late is often the fault of the client, here are some ways to make emotional labour easier.

Establish payment terms before you start writing
Thirty days is the norm, but make sure you check before you start writing. Payment on publication is a horrible beast, but some companies still insist upon it.

Invoice immediately
Don't dilly-dally with your invoicing. As soon as a piece has been accepted, send that invoice, with a day on the invoice when payment is due. Reiterate this date in the email. There's an invoice template on page 221.

Send the invoice separately
One of my bad habits is pitching my editors another piece and saying, 'Oh, and while I remember, here's my invoice for July!' Ten emails into a commission about flamingos and your invoice is completely lost.

Do all of your financial admin at the same time each week
Rather than letting your anxieties creep into little bits of your workday when you're in the middle of something important, stick to chasing clients and invoices at the same time each week. Call it a 'money hour'. Don't do it on a Friday afternoon, that's no way to start your weekend. If all of your clients have paid on time, glory be, take the hour off!

Chase as soon as payment is overdue
When it's late, it's late.

Don't count your money as yours until it's in your account

This is hard, but it's not your money until it's with you.

This sounds like a massive ball-ache, Sian, why can't I just ask for my money upfront?

If you're doing a long-term writing project, you absolutely can ask for some of your money upfront. It's far more common in copywriting. When you're commissioned for features, getting the money upfront is unlikely unless it's a long read that's going to take the best part of a year. If you're copywriting, suggest a model of payment similar to the one book publishers use – a third on acceptance, a third on completion of work and a third on completion of edits. Or a fifty-fifty split in the work. If you agree to get paid in advance, don't start the work until you've actually got the money.

I know that this all sounds exhausting. Chasing money is the worst bit about being freelance. But if you can keep on top of your finances and cashflow, it's manageable. It's also why the decisions I make aren't all money-based, and why I don't think happiness as a freelancer is entirely reliant on the figure on your invoices. Sometimes we have to perform tricks and jump through hoops just to get what we're owed. I don't want to do that for my happiness, so it has to come from elsewhere. There are so many more factors in accepting a project. Is there any point working with a client if you know they're going to be shady when it comes to payment? Sometimes you just have that feeling in the pit of your stomach that as soon as the work is wrapped up you won't see your client for dust (I once had a client invent a fake hospital emergency to get out of paying me). When you start a new project with a client, you should be totally sure your client is trustworthy. Trust your gut. You'll never regret not working with a client that might have caused huge amounts of anxiety. When you turn down work, you haven't lost anything; it's all hypothetical. You've only lost the money when you've started the work. Until then, what you've actually gained is space for clients that you love working with and who respect your time and your talent.

Freelance success story

'My definition of success as a freelance writer is pretty simple: to live comfortably from my work. Over the last eighteen years I've had moments where I've yearned for awards, seen my peers do 'better than' me, lamented the fact that I haven't had an editorship or written for some of the bigger publications out there. I allowed societal constructs of success to taint my view of my own career which has been a success in its own right. I grew up in a single-parent family, my mum was on benefits, and we lived on a council estate; back then I always dreamed of being able to afford anything I wanted and not having to worry about money so much. I'm kinda there now; not rich at all, but living frugally and earning enough to feel comfortable. That's success for me.'
Marcus Barnes, freelance music writer

Knowing your worth

Pricing your work can be complicated. There are some instances when you won't even have an option – a section editor's blanket rate is the only rate you'll get and whether you accept it is up to you.

So instead of asking what you should charge, think about how much you're worth. When you know that, you can find a rate that works for you, for all clients.

When you undersell yourself, it's because you didn't value your work enough.

I remember jumping on a brilliant commission for a new magazine that landed in my inbox one January (any commission that arrives in a quiet month is welcomed with open arms). Then I got started and realised that the work involved meant that I was making well below what I would usually charge. I was so happy to accept the commission and have a fun piece to write that I didn't stop to think about it. I had undervalued my work, and I should have asked for more money. I loved writing that feature and I was proud of it, but I was out of pocket and it was my own fault. It doesn't matter how many commissions you have under your belt, you can still make a rash decision. I wish I'd read through the brief a couple more times before hastily bashing 'YES PLEASE!!!' in reply. I should have taken a breath.

This article made me a bit grumbly for a couple of days, and knowing I should have asked for more took the edge off my enjoyment of the work. I may not have got more money, but that's not what's important – *I* knew that my time was worth more than I invoiced for. If you're accepting a huge copy job for less than you're worth, you might find that you've set yourself up for months of late nights that just aren't worth it. Now I try not to rush into things. The commission won't go anywhere in the time it takes you to make a cup of tea and read that email over one more time.

When any commission comes your way:

Clarify the specifics

The deadline, the word count and the rate. If you don't know these things, you're setting yourself up for a headache. It's on you to be very certain about these before getting started. Every time I've ignored this lesson (and I'm sorry to say it's been more than once), I've been burned.

If you think the rate is too low, speak up

Unless the parameters of a project change drastically, the rate you agree to is the rate you're getting so if you're not happy with it, say something.

But what's a good rate?

When it comes to pricing your work, you've got a couple of options. I charge at least £350 a day for most copywriting work. For features you'll probably be offered a word rate (anything over 40p per word is fairly good; I don't accept anything under 20p per word). You might also have to calculate a fee for an entire project, and this can be tricky – you're not just thinking in terms of day rates, but also your value and expertise. A client isn't just paying for the words in that article, they're paying for your years of experience, talent and knowledge.

What's particularly helpful is to know what your benchmarks are. What's your dream day rate? What's the rate you're happy working at for a sustained period of time? And lastly, what's the rate that you don't go a penny under? When you're clear on these, you can negotiate. I'll never forget the editor who told me I priced myself way too low for commercial copywriting work the day *after* she hired me. 'Never charge an agency less than £300 a day; our clients have got the money to spend.' She paid for drinks that night and I immediately increased my rate. Copywriting work with agencies is lucrative – they're paid directly by big-money commercial clients, so their budgets are high. Creative and design agencies regularly hire freelance writers, but the work usually has a quick turnaround so it's often given to a friend of a friend. The easiest way to find this work is by way of introduction or recommendation, but you can also polish up your portfolio and send it directly to the editorial director at the agency. You're playing the long game here, and you might not hear back for months, but it's worth it when you do.

When you're pricing your work, you need to factor in several things:

- The time it'll take you to do the work.
- Your expertise – be realistic about this when you're starting out, but don't sell yourself short.
- The amount you need to live well. Factor in shoes, holidays, ice cream and nice things because you are not a word robot.
- Holiday pay and sick pay. If you forget this, you're never going to make enough money to live on.
- Tax. If you're not factoring in your tax on your prospective salary, you're actually earning 20% less than you'd like to each year.

When what you're offered isn't enough

Turning down work is hard. We get it drummed into us that we should be grateful for any opportunity that comes our way and say yes to everything.

A few years ago, I pitched an idea about South American architecture. The platform loved the pitch but the editor asked me to secure an interview, possibly even travel over for the piece. Then I found out that the rate was much lower than I'd anticipated and certainly not worth the trip to the other side of the world.

Rather than just straight up say that it wasn't enough, I stalled and told my potential client that I couldn't secure the interview. I made myself look unprofessional when the issue wasn't with me.

When you're offered a fee that isn't feasible, don't be scared to ask for more (turn to page 195 for more about negotiating). If the proposed fee can't be increased for whatever reason, don't be scared to walk away or take your pitch elsewhere. It's very rare that a pitch only has one home. If one editor is keen, others will be too.

When you're asked what your rates are

This is a nifty little negotiating trick that's often used by people holding the budget. You have to show your hand first, and that often means you undercharge. If you are confident about your rates to begin with, this doesn't happen. You can always say that you have some flexibility, but someone else's budget shouldn't change how you value your work and your talent.

> *Freelance success story*
> *'Freelance success is finding joy in the work itself, rather than its external markers. That means more than just getting paid well for creative work. It means finding meaning in a variety of projects and all aspects of my freelance career, including the business side of it.*
>
> *When I used to work in-house, I defined success using extrinsic measures like money, job title and organisation. Now, I feel successful when I get to do work that challenges me, fulfils me creatively and when I work with clients or collaborators who treat me with respect and empathy.'*
> ***Anna Codrea-Rado, journalist, podcaster and campaigner***

211

How to save money when you're a freelance writer

We all have the best of intentions, but without a regular payday, your goal of saving hundreds of pounds every month is incredibly difficult. So here are some tips that will help you to save without stressing yourself out. I go for little and regular payments – sometimes so small I don't even notice them, but they all add up.

The 20% rule

Put 20% of every invoice that you get paid into a separate account. Saving for your tax bill really is this simple. Aim for 30% if you can.

Round things up

Some banks have the option to round up your pennies and pop them in your savings account. Whenever you use your debit card, in person or online, the change can be rounded up to the nearest pound. The debits are very little money at all – you were going to spend £2.99 on that bunch of supermarket daisies anyway – but over a week, a month, a year, those pennies add up to a pretty significant pot of cash.

Get things in (standing) order

Every week I have a standing order that goes into my savings account. It is the absolute minimum that my bank would allow me to set up (£10). I don't think about it, and because it's a small and regular payment, it's helped me save thousands of pounds without even noticing.

There's an app for that

Savings apps can divide opinion because you have to give read-only access to your bank account, which some people aren't comfortable with. However, I am all for them. The algorithms are clever and they only ever save what you can afford, so even if you're making less than you'd like, you can still save to pay off debts – this is how I cleared my overdraft. There are a few apps on the market, so do your research to pick the best for you. (I use Plum, which is great; Chip's customer service is resoundingly awful). This little app pays a large chunk of my tax bill each year.

Open a business account

You might find it helps to open a business account for all invoices and essentially pay yourself a salary from it. It'll certainly help when it comes to working out your expenses. That way you know what money you've made from freelancing, rather than that cheque in your birthday card from your nan.

Don't forget the treats

I am a huge believer in the Small Freelance Treat. Finished a difficult feature? Have a treat. Met a massive deadline? Treats for days. Finally sent the difficult email? Treaty treaty treats. My treat allowance is pretty significant, but even that's changed over the years. The buzz of a cheap pair of earrings isn't the same as it used to be. Cake is my usual treat because it's cheap and immediate and means I take a walk to the nice bakery, but I've realised that I get more lasting joy out of a beautiful book, or a pair of shoes I've had my eye on for ages. I don't deny myself treats – that's not what the freelance life is about – but I make sure it's something I really want.

Account for joy

Build a fund that's separate from your savings so you're not dipping into your tax pot or emergency account. Now you've already accounted for the vital things, this fund is for joy and joy alone. Give yourself permission to enjoy the money you earn. Always remember to account for joy.

The last word

If you only take one thing away from this chapter, focus on the fact that freelance writing is a business. When you start taking yourself seriously as a freelancer and get smart about your finances, doors open up.

Everything you do as a freelance writer is a lot easier when you're relaxed.

Having huge amounts of money in the bank is not the answer to being good with money. Don't wait until you're making £1 a word or commanding £400 a day before you start to take care of your finances or you replace the client who repeatedly pays you late. Do what you can today. The regular intention is so much more important than the amount.

That's what everything in this book is about. Regular commitments, small steps, deliberate actions. Deciding to do the hard work that makes your life easier, so you can focus on the things that make you happier. Success isn't about your bottom line. It's about taking control of your own happiness and choosing to put that first every single day. Allowing that intention to drive us is how we find our freelance and financial success.

The Final Word

When I started writing this book, I imagined it would end on a grand statement. A galvanising call to action. I don't think there is one, unless it's the collective action of hundreds of freelance writers putting the kettle on. There's no one moment where everything slots together nicely and you know that you've 'made it'. You're not Melanie Griffith in *Working Girl*. I wanted to be Joan Cusack anyway.

Your freelance writing career will remain a constant work in progress. You can plan and prepare and shoot for your goals and dreams, but you still don't know what opportunities you'll be presented with from one week to the next. None of it is set in stone. Therein lies the joy of freelance writing.

I still don't have all the answers. I'm lucky enough to surround myself with brilliant writers, editors and supportive friends who help me fill in the blanks and make me feel confident enough to navigate my way through the blind spots. What I do have is optimism for the future of writing as a career, and the future of how we choose to work.

I see more and more writers taking control of their careers, and their finances. It's not just life-changing, it's industry-changing. With that comes an undeniable shift in our society and our culture. I don't think our government understands or respects self-employment as a career choice, but there will soon come a time when that shift is impossible to ignore. Freelancing isn't an unusual lifestyle anymore. Our definition of a career ladder has changed. What we're striving for is very different to our aims a decade ago and our version of success is new, but that's OK, because we're the ones writing our future.

I hope this book inspires you to create a meaningful work life and a freelance writing career that you can define as successful on your own terms. I hope you'll be so bold that you'll surprise yourself and say yes to opportunities you couldn't have even imagined. I hope that you jump on your ideas and follow through on the 'what if?' that you had on a packed train. I hope that the work you do that no one sees – the spreadsheets, the drafts, the lists, the folders, the unsexy systems – helps you take a holiday every so often, and that you make time to celebrate your wins. Not just the big ones, but the small joys, too.

I hope you love your freelance life.

And I hope you write about it.

Resources

A freelancer does not create a career solo; we've got tricks and tools just like any other business. Here are the resources that I use on a regular basis. Don't forget, any fees for the tools and apps in this section can be expensed, as can membership to the organisations.

Newsletters

- *Freelance Writing Jobs* – my weekly jobs newsletter
- *LANCE* – run by Anna Codrea-Rado
- *Nikesh's Writing Tips* – a seasonal newsletter packed with writing advice from fellow Unbound author Nikesh Shukla; it leans towards fiction, but the advice is universally excellent
- *Sonder & Tell* – this industry newsletter is so brilliant at narrowing down what words can do and why choosing the right ones is so important
- *Storythings* – a weekly stream of inspiration
- *Talking Travel Writing* – if you want to be a travel writer, you should be signed up to this list

Books

- *Big Magic: How to Live a Creative Life, and Let Go of Your Fear,* Elizabeth Gilbert
- *On Writing: A Memoir of the Craft,* Stephen King
- *The Right to Write: An Invitation and Initiation into the Writing Life,* Julia Cameron
- *Tips from a Publisher: A Guide to Writing, Editing, Submitting and Publishing Your Book,* Scott Pack
- *Where Good Ideas Come From: The Natural History of Innovation,* Steven Johnson
- *You're the Business: How to Build a Successful Career When You Strike Out Alone,* Anna Codrea-Rado

Tools and apps

Feedly
Collect article feeds from websites that you use regularly so that you can keep up with the latest news and trends in your industry.

Google Alerts
Yes, obviously you're going to set up a Google Alert for your own name, but you should also be setting up alerts for search terms about your own niche and expertise, too. Let the stories come to you!

PicMonkey
A reasonably priced browser image editor. If you can't afford Photoshop, it's worth paying £50 a year for.

Pocket

Pocket is the app I use more than anything else. I save so many articles, jobs, shoes I like, tweets from editors looking for pitches, and refer back when I'm ready. If your bookmarks are out of control, you need this. It changed my life.

Scrivener

I wrote this book on Scrivener. I use it for any large project I write. It's pretty cheap, and the free trial only runs down on the days you use it.

Self Control

Got a deadline? Use this browser extension to lock yourself out of those distracting websites. It'll keep running even if you turn your computer off and on. There's a similar Mac app that goes by the same name.

TweetDeck

Set up the searches you need in separate columns, rather than doing a manual search.

Organisations

Cision

The best company for sending out PR requests. Find out more about how to do this on page 60.

IPSE
The Association of Independent Professionals and the Self-Employed. A non-profit organisation that helps freelancers and self-employed professionals across all industries develop and sustain their careers.

NCTJ
The National Council for the Training of Journalists. A lot of news organisations ask for you to be NCTJ-qualified.

NUJ
The National Union of Journalists. There's a freelance arm to this professional union.

ResponseSource
Another useful media connection company.

Society of Freelance Journalists
An international community of freelance journalists, editors and content creators.

Not sure how to lay out your first invoice? Here's a template.

Sian Meades-Williams
12 Chapter Gardens
Writers Lane
London
N1 YAY

+44 (0) 000 0000 000
youremailaddress@email.com

31 December 2026 *The date is crucial! Your payment terms count down from this date.*

INVOICE: PJM-SMW001 *Number your invoices to each client so they're easier for you to track.*

Purchase/job number: 123456 *Some clients might have their own job or PO numbers that they need you to reference. Ask for this before you start the work, otherwise you might find that you're waiting weeks to send your invoice.*

F.A.O. Very Nice Editor *Include a point of contact in case anything needs checking.*

Client name *Always use the company name, not just the name of the publication you featured in.*
Publication name
108 Make Me Rich Avenue
London
WC1 1££

Description:
Add a single line about your work, and include the rate for each line item. Make sure you include the publication date, link or issue number.

Brilliant article that got you hundreds of page views and only one angry comment.
12.11.26 – £240

Dazzling feature about bees. Issue 15. £400.

Grand total: £640

Payment Details:
Sian Meades-Williams
Moneybags bank
Account number: 12345678
Sort Code: 12-34-56

If you're working with companies abroad, they may also ask for your IBAN and Swift numbers. Both should be on your bank statements or online banking.

Payment to be made via the agreed payment method within 30 days of invoice. Late payments will be subject to a late payment fee and interest will be charged.

Even if you don't include this statement, legally it still stands.

Glossary

B2B: business to business. It's important that you know who your client is targeting. If not B2B, it's…

B2C: business to consumer.

box outs: the little boxes of copy that you see in magazines for facts and bitesize information.

brief: the document that you want from your editor/client to tell you exactly what you're writing.

byline: woohoo, your name up in lights! Or in print, at least.

clips: your writing samples. They can be PDFs or links to your work online.

CMS: content management system. Whatever platform you're using to upload content to a website. It might be Wordpress or Squarespace or a custom-built platform. Each has their own quirks and foibles.

cold pitch: emailing a potential client with no prior contact or introduction. Not as scary as it sounds, find out more in the 'Getting Work' chapter.

copy: just a fancy way of referring to any words you write.

copyright: the owner of your work. In some cases, copyright stays with the writer and the work is licensed so that it can be published, but some publishing companies insist that the copyright belongs to them. Make sure you check this.

evergreen: a topic that's good all year round. These are particularly good for SEO (search engine optimisation – see later in the list).

flat-plan: the layout of a magazine that gives a rundown of every article and advert.

filing: sending your finished copy to your editor.

hook: the reason people will want to read your piece. Usually the hook is something news-related.

IBAN: International Bank Account Number. If you're working for a company abroad, they might ask you for your IBAN so they can pay you. It'll be on your bank statement.

invoice: the document you send to your client in order to get paid (check out page 221 for an example).

kill fee: the fee you'll get if an editor commissions your piece but ends up not running it. It's usually somewhere between 25–50% of the agreed fee.

lede: the introduction to a story.

NDA: non-disclosure agreement. Sometimes, especially when working with agencies and commercial clients, you'll need to sign an NDA before you can discuss a potential project.

on spec: when an editor asks you to write an entire piece before they decide if they're going to pay for it.

op-ed: traditionally the op-ed was the comment piece that sat opposite the editor's letter. Now it's shorthand for opinion pieces.

par: media people say par instead of paragraph. Happens most often in newspapers.

PAYE: pay as you earn. When you work regularly on magazines or newspapers, a PAYE payment system where you input your own hours is likely. Your company will handle the tax.

payment on acceptance: a growing number of publications will allow you to invoice as soon as they've accepted your work.

payment on account: the upfront payment added to your tax bill each year so you're not paying in arrears. You can read more about this on page 184.

payment on publication: perhaps the worst of all the payment terms – a publisher could hold onto your unpublished feature for months, or even years, without ever paying you for it.

payment terms: the length of time a client has to pay your invoice. Usually, it's thirty days. Sometimes it'll be sixty days (or worse, ninety).

peg: similar to 'hook', you peg a story onto something newsworthy.

pitch: your brilliant idea, laid out clearly for a potential client/editor.

portfolio: if you've done a lot of copy work with brands, it helps for you to have a PDF portfolio or your work.

pull quote: choice bits of copy that are pulled from your article and highlighted on the page to draw readers in.

retainer: a regular amount a client pays for your time, whether they end up needing you or not. Lovely.

SEO: search engine optimisation. Using crucial search terms and keywords in your work can help boost an article's rankings on Google. It's not as trendy as it used to be (and Google changes the rules around it so people can't 'game' the system), but getting to know the basics is useful.

style guide: wondering if your client uses the Oxford comma or caps up every word of their headline? Hopefully they'll have a style guide that will tell you. Pay attention to it, otherwise you're just going to get a lot of fiddly edits.

TK: weirdly, this means 'to come'. It signifies when there's a photo or extra copy to be inserted. Why not 'TC', you wonder? You're far less likely to use TK in your document, rather than TC – nutcracker, matchmaker, witchcraft – so it's much easier to search for.

vertical: a massive internet buzzword that we don't use so much anymore. It just means the section of a website.

Sources

1 Chloe Jepps, *What Makes a Freelancer?*, IPSE, 12 January 2020, available at www.ipse.co.uk/resource/what-makes-a-freelancer.html

2 IPSE, *The Self-Employed Landscape Report 2019*, 2019, available at www.ipse.co.uk/policy/research/the-self-employed-landscape/the-self-employed-landscape-report-2019.html

3 Inna Yordanova, *Women in Self-Employment*, IPSE, 9 March 2020, available at www.ipse.co.uk/resource/women-in-self-employment.html

4 Elizabeth Gilbert, *Big Magic: How to Live a Creative Life, and Let Go of Your Fear*, Bloomsbury, London, 2015.

5 Carmen Nobel, 'Professional networking makes people feel dirty', Working Knowledge, Harvard Business School, 9 February 2015, available at hbswk.hbs.edu/item/professional-networking-makes-people-feel-dirty

6 Ethan Kross, Marc G. Berman, et al., 'Social rejection shares somatosensory representations with physical pain', PNAS, 22 February 2011, available at www.pnas.org/content/108/15/6270

7 Kim Liao, 'Why you should aim for 100 rejections a year', Lit Hub, 28 June 2016, available at lithub.com/why-you-should-aim-for-100-rejections-a-year

8 Melissa Febos, 'Do you want to be known for your writing, or for your swift email responses?', Catapult, 23 March 2017, available at catapult.co/stories/do-you-want-to-be-known-for-your-writing-or-for-your-swift-email-responses

9 Suzanne Bearne, 'Self-employed? Here's what you should do about pensions', *Guardian*, 11 January 2020, available at www.theguardian.com/money/2020/jan/11/self-employed-what-to-do-about-pensions

10 Inna Yordanova, *Women in Self-Employment*, IPSE, 9 March 2020, available at www.ipse.co.uk/resource/women-in-self-employment.html

11 Mark Spilsbury, *Exploring Freelance Journalism*, NCTJ, December 2016, available at www.nctj.com/downloadlibrary/EXPLORING%20FREELANCE%20JOURNALISM%20FINAL.pdf

Acknowledgements

There's an astonishing number of people involved in making a book a reality and that's even more true with an Unbound publication. Sincerest thank yous to every single one of my supporters, who believed in *The Pyjama Myth* when it was just a nugget of an idea. This book exists because of you.

Enormous thanks go to the whole team at Unbound, but especially to DeAndra Lupu, Rachael Kerr, Hayley Shepherd, Katy Guest and John Mitchinson. A special mention to Georgia Odd and, of course, my dazzling commissioning editor Fiona Lensvelt, who replied with such joy and enthusiasm to the pitch I sent at 1 a.m. and remained joyful and enthusiastic throughout the entire process. I'm delighted to have such a brilliant bunch of cheerleaders.

I mention in the book that freelancers get to choose their own colleagues and I'm so lucky that mine include Laura Brown – my *Tigers Are Better Looking* co-editor and favourite person in the whole of Scotland – and my freelance partner in crime Anna Codrea-Rado. I'm also hugely grateful to Gemma Cartwright and Frances Ambler for their endless writing chat and support that goes back much further than my first draft.

Sometimes kindness comes at the most unexpected times. Not least from Jess Love, an absolute treasure who posted me salt-and-vinegar Squares when I met my first deadline, and Gemma Milne – who knew exactly when I was floundering, and also knew exactly what to say.

I also have endless gratitude to every writer, editor and expert who gave me their time and input for this book. Your wisdom and generosity are incredible. I've learned so much from you all; I hope other writers do, too.

I happen to be writing this page on the morning of my husband's birthday. So, Tom, thank you for your intelligence and care with my drafts, an estimated 37,289 cups of tea since records began, your patience when I was writing all the wrong words, and your unending support when I decided to send a book pitch at 1 a.m. the week before our wedding. Thank you for encouraging me to keep writing and for making every day an adventure, even if we're just frying eggs. Happy birthday.

A Note on the Author

Sian Meades-Williams is a freelance writer with more than fifteen years' experience in replying to emails and chasing invoices. She's written for *The Times*, *Style*, the *New York Times*, and *The Simple Things* and co-edits the lifestyle newsletter *Tigers Are Better Looking*. Alongside her popular media industry newsletter, *Freelance Writing Jobs*, she's also co-founder of the Freelance Writing Awards. She lives in Islington, North London, with her husband Tom and her naughty tabby cat Chip.

www.sianmeadeswilliams.com
@SianySianySiany

A Note on the Author

Unbound is the world's first crowdfunding publisher, established in 2011.

We believe that wonderful things can happen when you clear a path for people who share a passion. That's why we've built a platform that brings together readers and authors to crowdfund books they believe in – and give fresh ideas that don't fit the traditional mould the chance they deserve.

This book is in your hands because readers made it possible. Everyone who pledged their support is listed below. Join them by visiting unbound.com and supporting a book today.

Kelly Ballard
Amelia Banks
Nicola Bannock
Rachel Barber
Mark Barden
Becky Barnes
Marcus Barnes
Alice Barnes-Brown
Bianca Barratt
Shannon Barrett
Zena Barrie
Marisa Bate
Navaz Batliwalla
Emma Batrick
Sarah Baxter
Rob Beadle
Rachael Beale
Natalie Becher
Emily Beecher
James Beeken
Eliot Beer
Emily Benita
Jane Bentley
Lucy Benton
Luc Benyon
Tristan Bernays
Dale Berning Sawa
Lindsey Berthoud
Bella Binns
Danny Birchall
KV Birkett-Stubbs

Bryony Bishop
Katie Bishop
Laurence Bisot
Vanessa Bissessur
Karin Blak
Vikki Blake
Cara Bland
Abigail Blasi
Keeley Bolger
Joanna Booth
Sara Booth
Theo Bosanquet
Liz Bourne
Anna Bowen
Ed Bowsher
Luke Bowyer
Julie Boyne
Katy Bravery
Lauren Bravo
Penny Brazier
Fiona Brennan
Stephanie Bretherton
Simon Brew
Jacq Bridge
Mark Bridge
Megan-Elizabeth
  Bridges
Kimberly Bright
Rebecca Broad
Laura Broadbent
Alice Broadribb

Holly Brockwell
Jenni Brodie
Kristian Brodie
Amy Brooke
Iain Broome
Alice Broster
Beverley Brown
Francesca Brown
Joanna Brown
Kat Brown
Laura Brown
Lauren Brown
Lorraine Browne
Megan Brownrigg
Anne Bruce
Celia Bryan-Bryan
Julia Buckley
Seth Burgess
Ian Burke
Emma Burnell
Alexandra Burton
Stephanie Butler
Ianthe Butt
Caroline Butterwick
Charlotte Buxton
Lily C
Becca Caddy
Ian Calcutt
Ed Callow
Corrie Campbell
Laura Cappelle

Cardiff University School
    of Journalism
Carmel Cardona
Hannah Carlyon
Gemma Cartwright
Eleni Cashell
Charlotte Cassedanne
Michelle Chai
Mike Challis
Darryl Chamberlain
Raphael Chapell
Hayley Chappell
Andrew Charlton
Anita Chaudhuri
Chloe Chittenden
Matt Chittock
Polina Chizhova
Katie Clark
Penny Clark
Sarah Clark
Amy Clarke
Clare Clarke
Rosie Clarke
Ross Clarke
Verity Clarke
Victoria Clarke
Anna Claybourne
Melanie Clegg
Megan Clement
Ed Clews
Siseley Coates-Harman

Vanessa Cobb

Anna Codrea-Rado

Sally Coffey

Will Coldwell

Barry Collins

Simon Columb

Amy Condron

Kirsty Connell-Skinner

Selina Conroy

Kathryn Conway

Jude Cook

Bridget Cordy

Karen Cornish

Emma Coxon

Dawn Coxwell

Andy Coyle

Helen Craig

Emma Creese

Lucy Crehan

Portia Crowe

Suzanna Cruickshank

Mary R. Crumpton

Briony Cullin

Trisha D'Hoker

Sara D'Souza

Malika Dalamal

Sarah-Jane Dale

Katie Dancey-Downs

Jane Darroch Riley

Meera Dattani

Charlotte Davey

Karen Davidson

Amy Davies

Ceri Davies

Emily Davies

Maxine Davies

Will Davies

Jack Davy

Sarah Dawson

Tom de Castella

Marthe de Ferrer

Aina de Lapparent

Paula Dear

Andrew Deathe

AJ Dehany

Lizzy Dening

Melissa Dennis

Daf Dent

Melanie Denyer

Rohese Devereux Taylor

Andrew Dickens

Alice Diggory

Frank Dillon

Poppy Dinsey

Hannah Donaldson

Stephen Doswell

Charlotte Dougall

Kevin Dowling

Stella Downey

Sarah Drumm

DSP

Charlotte Duff

Frances Durkin
Jamie Dwelly
Kathryn Eastman
Florence Eastoe
Cariad Eccleston
Isobel Edwards
Katie Edwards
Tom Ellett
Jemima Elliott
Laura Elliott
Mark Elliott
Ben Ellis
Lucy Ellis
Jess Ellison
Emma Elobeid
Joff Elphick
Natalie Elvin
Jill Emeny
Ruth Emery
Eris (they/them)
Firgas Esack
Jan Evans
Kate Evans
Sara Evans
Sarah Evans
Rebecca Evelyn Barnes
Elyssa Fagan
Priya Faith
Julie Farrell
Rosaleen Fenton
Lisa-Marie Ferla

Veronica Ferrari
Laura Fewell
Jamie Fewery
Andrew Fisher
Joseph Flaig
Gary Flood
Pádraig Floyd
Anna Foden
Steve Folland
Julia Forster
Lois Forster
Jenny Foster
Laura Fountain
Clare Fowler
Audrey Fox
Cass Fox
Anna Francis
Oliver Franklin-Wallis
Lisa Franks
Elska Franzen
Mick Freed
Becky Freeth
Vitalija Freitakaite
John Frewin
Sam Fry
Ashley Fryer
Sophie Gadd
Alex Galbinski
Claire Gamble
Sarah Gane
Laura Garcia

Katherine Garrett

Lyndsey Garrett

Beth Garrod

Emily Garside

Sharon Gedney

Tom George

Woohoo Laura Ghost

Fiona Gibson

Sarah Giles

Susan Giles

Jennifer Gilmour

Victoria Glass

Sally Glover

Melissa Jenna Godsey

Clare Gogerty

Suzanne Goldberg

Sam Gonçalves

Zoey Goto

Leah Grant

Nick Gray

Sarah Green

Genevieve Greenhalgh

Hannah Greenstreet

Charlotte Griffiths

Tim Grindell

Jon Gripton

Imogen Groome

Lottie Gross

Simon Guerrier

Kate Guest

Katy Guest

Clare Gunn

Kevin Gurton

Sarah Hagger-Holt

Francesca Haig

Jen Haken

Rachael Hale

Jessica Hall

Kate Hall

Rebekah Hall

Patricia Hammond

Sally Hampton

Kyra Hanson

Steve Harcourt

Kathryn Harding

Natasha Harding

Laura Harker

Phoebe Harkins

Alice Harman

Louise Harman

Theresa Harold

Mike Harper Lee

Scheenagh Harrington

Harry Harris

Sally Harrop

Gillian Harvey

Kate Harvey

Dave Haste

Rebecca Hastings

Sophie Haydock

Gavin Haynes

Abbie Headon

Natalie Healey
Rachael Healy
Georgia Heath
Samuel Hedley
Michelle Hemstedt
Greg Henley
Anne Henry
Dan Hett
Leila Hewetson
Emily Hibbs
David Hillier
Donna Hillyer
Ana Hine
Matthew Hirtes
Charlie Hobson
James Edward Hodkinson
Sigrun Hodne
Kyle Hoekstra
Laura Hogevold
Helen Holmes
Kate Holmes
Nicholas Holmes
Mark Hood
Claire Hool
James Hopkirk
Peter Houston
Claire Hovey
Holly Howe
David Howell
Alice Hughes
Emma Hughes

Clair Humphries
Ali Hunter
Laura Hunter-Thomas
Qais Hussain, Bradford
Pamela Hutchinson
Claire Hutchison
Alice Hutton
Kay Hyde
Julian Hynd
Becca Inglis
Grace Irvine
Anita Isalska
Linde Jacobs
Minerva Jaquier
Celia Jenkins
Justine Jenkins
Lisa Jenkins
David Jesson
Kat John
Lauren John
Alexandra Johnson
Dan Johnson
Jess Johnson
Natalie Johnson
Sophie Johnson
Amy Jones
Danielle Jones
Elizabeth Jones
Ffion Jones
Katie Jones
Sammy Jones

Grainne Jordan

Emma Jordan (dgtlwriter)

Julie Joy

Alex Juras

Maya Kaiser

Liz Kalaugher

Amanda Kavanagh

Hannah Kaye

Breandán Kearney

Stevie Keen

Mandi Keighran

Andrej Kelemen

Hilary Kemp

Tristan Kennedy

Ian Kenworthy

Liz Kershaw

Dan Kieran

Anna Kierstan

Megan Kirby

Tom Kirby

Cherrie Kishazy

Torill Kornfeldt

Emilie Kristensen-McLachlan

Martin Kudlac

Ivana Kurecic

Anthea Lacchia

Marina Lai

Yvette Lamb

Anna Lambert

Teresa Lander

Callum Langston-Bolt

Anna Lao-Kaim

Kate Latham

Ariane Laurent-Smith

Will "ill Will" Lavin

Roz Laws

Shalaka Laxman

Caroline le Marechal

Kate Lee

Kelsey Lee Jones

Emma Lee-Potter

Fiona Lensvelt

Richard Leonard

Isobel Lewis

Perri Lewis

Sarah Lillywhite

Paul Linggood

Bronwen Livingstone

Helen Lock

Martin Locock

Dan Long

Charlotte Lorimer

Sarah Lothian

Jess Love

Nicola Love

Rebecca Low

Bridget Lubbock

Tilly Lunken

Roger Lytollis

Rosemary Mac Cabe

Leanne Macardle

Russell Mackintosh

Alistair Maclenan

Kyle MacNeill

Sarah Macpherson

Fiona Mactaggart

Laura Madeleine

Abigail Malbon

Fani Mari

Sarah Marland

Amy Marsden

Miss Harriet Marsden

Rachel Marsden

Georgia Marsh

Kaz Marston

Alex Marten

Natalie Martin

Mary

Catrin Mascall

Louise Maskill

Graeme Mason

Nicola Masters

Sofia Matias

Janina Matthewson

Mike Maurer

Lizzy Mayell

Dayna McAlpine

Olivia McCarthy

Amina McCauley

Ali McClary

Bethan McConnell

Mark McConville

Kelly McFarland

Julia McGee-Russell

Marie McGinley

Vanessa McGreevy

Keith McGuinness

Thomas McLachlan

Evelyn Mclaughlin

Brian Mcleish

James McMahon

Sean McManus

Lauren McMenemy

Pat McNulty

Mia McTigue-Rodriguez

Ailsa McWhinnie

Alan Meades

Sian Meades-Williams

Megha Merani

Leonie Mercedes

Jodie Merritt

Chloe Metzger

Anna Mewes

Anya Meyerowitz

James Middleton

Carol Miers

Hollie Miller

Lucy Miller

Richard Miller

Rachel Mills

Gemma Milne

Josh Minister

Harriet Minter

Beatriz Miranda

Veronique Mistiaen

Hilary Mitchell

Jackie Mitchell

John Mitchinson

Adam Moliver

Dee Montague

Charlotte Moore

James Moran

Jess Morgan

Amanda Moron-Garcia

Mary Morris

Sebastian Moss

Madeleine Mosse

Breanna Mroczek

Suzanne Mucci

Joerg Mueller-Kindt

Catherine Munson-Klein

Emily Murray

Kirsten Murray

Alexander Murray-Watters

Justin Myers

David Myles

Chitra Nagarajan

Karla Napoleon

Stu Nathan

Carlo Navato

Joy Nazzari

Graeme Neill

Zoe Neill

Iona Nelson

Jodie Nesling

Steve Newman

Lindy Newns

Matt Ng

Hazel Nicholson

Michelle Nicol

Daniel Nixon

Jenni Nock

Luke Norman

John Nugent

Jenni Nuttall

Kate O'Connor

Caoimhe O'Gorman

Marina O'Loughlin

Mark O'Neill

John-Michael O'Sullivan

Frank O'Mahony

Helen Ochyra

Jenny Oldaker

Matt Oliver

Tasha Onwuemezi

Leon Oteng

Suzi Ovens

Paul Oxberry

Scott Pack

Catherine Paice

Chris Park

Rianna Parker

Rich Parkinson-Williams

Steve Parks

Abby Parsons

Katie Partridge

Gopesh Deep Pathak

Zina Pearce-Tomenius

Lucy Pearson

Jenny Peebles

Dan Peeke

Kate Peers

Eleanor Pender

Manfreda Penfold

Katy Penman

Joanna Penn

Seth Pereira

Tiffany Philippou

Tom Phillips

Victoria Philpott

Wibbly Pig

Graeme Piper

Libby Plummer

Justin Pollard

Laura Pollard

Tracey Pollard

Mary-Anne Pontikis

Emily Powell

Ken Preston

Laura Price

Sian Price

Lucy Pritchard

Tom Pritchard

Daniel Puddicombe

Alice-May Purkiss

Georgie Pursey

Fiona Quinn

Alexa Radcliffe-Hart

Afreen Rahman

G. Ramazzotti

Alex Ramsden

Kayleigh Rattle

Linnie Rawlinson

Shona Ray Ferguson

Sharn Rayment

Kathryn Reay

Emma Reed

Claire Rees

Vicki Reeve

Yuan Ren

Catherine Renton

Rachael Revesz

Danielle Richardson

Anna Richardson Taylor

Olly Ricketts

Jennifer Riddalls

Andrea Rieger

Rae Ritchie

Julianne Robertson

Katrina Robinson

Alma Roda-Gil

Caroline Roddis

Laura Roddy

Jenny Rollen Picking

Sarah Ronan

Keira Esse Roth

Stephen Rötzsch Thomas

Lucinda Rouse

Jenny Rowe

Rachael Rowe

Miriam Rune

Lindsey Russell

Kate Ryan

Priya S

Katy Salter

Rochelle Sampy

Vanessa Sanders

Laura Sant

Nigel Sarbutts

Hannah Sargeant

Ros Sargent

Defne Saricetin

Beth Saunders

Shrikant Sawant

Abi Scaife

Louise Scarce

Joanna Scutts

Amy Sedghi

Rose Sgueglia

Diyora Shadijanova

Sooraj Shah

Liz Shankland

Christian Sharp

Becky Sheaves

Alicia Sheber

Marie Sheel

Philip Sheldrake

Alexandra Sheppard

Emma Sheppard

Diane Shipley

John Shirlaw

Anna Sikorska

Isabella Silvers

Nikki Simpson

Jill S Sinclair

Ally Sinyard

Leona Skene

Nicola Slawson

Daniel Slee

Ellie Slee

Jenna Sloan

Rebecca Slowley

Christine Smallwood

Alex MJ Smith

Ellie Smith

Fi Smith

Helena Smith

Ian Smith

Isobel Smith

Lyndsey Smith

Sarah Smith

Stacey Smith

Alice Snape

Giuseppe Sollazzo @puntofisso

Emma Southon

Emma Sparks

Carla Speight

Lucy Spencer

Sarah Spenser

Beth Squires

Paul Squires

Wendy Staden

Jenny Stallard

Jason B. Standing

Maureen Stapleton

Adam Stephens

Jennifer Still

Edward Stobbart

Emma Stokes

Bethan Stone

Lottie Storey

India Stoughton

Helen Sumbler

Ruth Summers

Chris Sutcliffe

Graeme Swanson

Claire Sweeting

Helen Tarver

Gabriel Tate

Emma Taylor

Gemma Taylor

Richard Taylor

Rhona Tennant

Felicity Theaker

Charlie Thomas

Andrew Thompson

Fiona Thompson

Julia Thompson

Andrew Tilbury

Darren Tilby

Matthew Tiller

Lydia Titman

Giles Todd

Borislava Todorova

Amy Toledano

Mitchell Tolliday

Jamie Tomkins

Graham Tomlinson

Francesca Tortora

Ellen Tout

Angela Tran

James Trew

Natalie Trice

Jake Tucker

Jenny Tudor

Giles Turnbull

Eleanor Turney

Wendy Tuxworth

Jessica Twentyman

Aisling Twomey

Art UK

Helen Underhill

Mitya Underwood

Anna Vall

Olivia Vandyk

R.B. Velebny

Regina Volkmer

Eliza W

Damon L. Wakes

Ellen Wallwork

Eleanor Walsh

Grace Walsh

Susan Walters

Kate Walton

Christian Ward

Mandy E Ward

Simon Ward

Ali Warner

Joanne Warnock

Nicola Washington

Sophia Waterfield

Jo Waters

Lara Watson

Tanya Weaver

Jonathan Weinberg

Sabrina Weiss

Anne Welsh

Rhian Westbury

Robin Weston

Louise Whitbread

Emma Whitehall

Lucy Whitehouse

Ben Whitelaw

Philip Whiteley

Shirley Whiteside

Claire Whittaker

Sean Whittington Roy

Lidia Molina Whyte

Diane Wild

Katherine Wildman

Sam Wilkinson

Venetia Wilks

Holly Williams

Isaac Williams

Jenessa Williams

Rosmund Williams

Tom Williams

Julie Williamson

Julia Wills

Jesse Wilson

Sam Winkler

Emma Winterschladen

Ellie Wood

Sarah Wood

Lottie Woodrow

Monica Woods

Danielle Woodward

Michelle Worthington

Becky Wren

Alice Wright

Eleanor Wright

Emma Wright

Jack Wynn

Melanie Yorke

Stephanie Young

Paula Younger

Anna Zammit

Alan Zoldan

With special thanks to IPSE for their generous support of this book